D J Dodds
January 1996

Robert Woolley

Going

A MEMOIR OF ART, SOCIETY, AND CHARITY

Once

SIMON & SCHUSTER

New York   London   Toronto

Sydney   Tokyo   Singapore

SIMON & SCHUSTER
Rockefeller Center
1230 Avenue of the Americas
New York, NY 10020

Designed by Jeanette Olender

Photo insert designed by Paula R. Szafranski

Manufactured in the United States of America

10   9   8   7   6   5   4   3   2   1

Library of Congress Cataloging-in-Publication Data
Woolley, Robert, date.
Going once : a memoir of art, society, and charity / Robert Woolley.
p. cm.   Includes index.
1. Woolley, Robert, date.
2. Auctioneer—United States—Biography.
I. Title.
N8604.W66A3   1995   709'.2—dc20
[B]   95-33604   CIP

ISBN 0-684-81385-8

For Dede and David

Contents

Foreword

Over two years ago, Charles Gwathmey, the renowned architect, and his wife, Bette-Ann, stopped me in a restaurant and told me their son, Eric Steel, wanted to have lunch with me. As an openly gay man, I rarely find my dates through their parents. I met Eric a few days later. He's an attractive man in his early thirties, and it turned out that he was an editor at Simon & Schuster. Eric wanted to meet me because I had been the subject of a feature article in the January 1993 issue of *Vanity Fair.* Eric had read it, and he said, "There's a book in you." And for the next two years he called me faithfully to remind me about the book.

I told my friends about my intentions, and over time people would say, "How's the book coming?"

I always said that it was finished. "I just have to write it down."

I have finally written it down. Thank you, Eric.

Prologue

Nothing is more distracting than falling in love with an object—a painting, a silver vessel—nothing is more beguiling than bidding for it against others who love it too. As an auctioneer, I have been making this happen for the last twenty-five years. As the head of decorative arts at Sotheby's, I have touched some of the most beautiful and valuable objects in the world: Fabergé eggs, Medici porcelain, cloissoné enamel, royal French furniture.

As best I could, I have made sure that the object that belongs to the consignor on the right moves to the buyer on the left. It's really a very simple philosophical role, and yet it is so much more than just being a middleman. I conduct a careful orchestration of players: experts, financial advisers, and Teamsters, whose collective efforts finally bring the object before a crowd trembling with desire.

Now I have taken my position at Sotheby's and have created my own special performance art. They call me the Fantasy Auctioneer, the merchant of the dream bazaar. Come to my auctions, and I will sell you an expensive favor that may never be available again: dinner with the mayor of New York, a walk-on role in a Woody Allen movie, your swimming pool painted by David Hockney. But there will be only a few moments to decide, and a reckless bid may or may not grant you that wish. If you ask me how much you should spend for something at auction, I'll tell you to reach for the point of pain, where if you have to shell out one dime more you'll go completely mad. If you are victorious, my congratulations; if you lose, then I'll remind you that your best collection of objects is the list of things that you almost bought.

My love of art is profane, not sacred. The sacred love of art belongs to museums, which are concerned more with verifying dates than with finding values. At Sotheby's, although we generally get the dates right, we look for that combination of object and estimate that will transform the auction hall into a swirl of activity, for the object that will make prospective bidders say to themselves, "This has to be mine." I've always said that collecting at Sotheby's is the penultimate act. The ultimate act, of course, is dying.

I know that all too well, because I've reached my own point of pain, the moment where the bidding has slowed and I truly don't know how many moments I have left until the gavel comes down. Perhaps it's more elegant to say I've rounded the arc of my ascent.

I am fifty years old, and I'm writing this now because I have AIDS. If some of us were slated to live immortally, then dying would truly be a bitch. But we are all in this final act together, and the law of life is that each of us will, at some point, be where I am now. In an ironic way, I suppose the terminal "we" have a better sense of what's left. But we also know the value of true distraction.

As I see it, there are three types of people who acquire art and objects: collectors, accumulators, and furnishers. Collectors are people with theme and passion who will sell their mother for the missing link in their chain of acquisitions. Accumulators are people who will pile on as much as they can of many different things. Although some aesthetes have said "less is more," accumulators know that "more is more"—it's as simple as that. I am definitely a member of this club. Furnishers buy to fit a certain scheme. They're looking for a painting to match a console to match a sofa, and as soon as they're finished with one project, they're on to the next aesthetic challenge. Perhaps "aesthetically challenged" is the perfect politically correct name for interior decorators—or designers, as they prefer to be called—as well as for anyone on a budget. For the purest form of acquisition is never hindered by the issue of money.

Investment should never be the primary motive for collecting. If you bought something for $1,000 ten years ago and it's now worth $10,000, you will probably claim to be an art investor. If, however, you paid $10,000 ten years ago for something that is now worth only $1,000, you will call yourself a collector. If you become an investor, it's an accident of fate. In my nearly thirty years in the art business, there's only one circumstance I know of where art was bought strictly as an investment to be resold. And the company that invested made only a 6.9 percent return on its money. The people there were smart too—they probably would've done as well on Wall Street or at a bank.

I believe that people should become true collectors at that stage in their life when they finally get their money together. In the most modest of circumstances, this would be when the kids have finished their education, which has been paid for, and the house mortgage has been winnowed down. But for most people who buy at Sotheby's, paying for Johnny's tuition or for the beach house is usually the least of their expenses.

Auction house exhibitions are almost always a great educational tool. For one thing, unlike museums, which will cut off your hand if you so much as reach toward a display case, auction houses will allow you to handle the inventory and inspect it closely. Auction houses will give you a catalog that distills a description of each particular object; tell you the date when it was made and who owned it, if there is an available nugget of history; and, of course, give you an estimate of price that was calculated by an expert. If you ask the right questions of the right people at an auction house, you can learn a lot more than you think.

However, as far as serious collecting is concerned, people must begin with what attracts them. Seek out the advice of experts. A professor of medieval art, or a curator of Islamic manuscripts, whose expertise is sought relatively seldom, might happily oblige. Mistakes will be made, especially in the beginning, and over a period of time tastes change. Something you loved twenty years ago may presently make you wonder why you ever bought it. And yet it would make sense that these inanimate *objets de vertu* are, in the end, not much different from the objects of our affection. We tire of things, we tire of people. Don't get me wrong—I'm not advocating collecting over love, although I know many people who believe that at least they will never be deserted by their collections.

I don't think I would be writing this book but for the events that transpired on a certain day in July of 1987, one of the most miserable twenty-four-hour periods of my life. I had inadvertently booked myself to work two auctions: one, at Sotheby's in Manhattan, a morning and afternoon session comprising some five hundred lots of European works of art; the other a benefit auction for the Parrish Art Museum, ninety miles east of Manhattan in Southampton, Long Island. If everything ran smoothly in my Sotheby's auction, I would have just enough time to get into a car and drive through the blistering heat on the overly busy, traditionally bumper-to-bumper Long Island Expressway. Unfortunately, the afternoon session of European art took a lot longer than usual, and at 5:00 P.M. I was still gaveling. There was nothing I could do but call the Parrish Museum, and they arranged with one of their wealthy patrons to send a private plane to meet me at La Guardia Airport.

But more important than this time crunch was the fact that my lover of fourteen years, Jeffrey Childs, was at that moment lying in our apartment, dying from a kind of brain fever that is one of AIDS's unassailable afflictions. The last thing I wanted to be doing on that Saturday afternoon was to ride out to La Guardia in the back of a taxicab. But I had committed myself to doing this auction months in advance, and I had helped with its creation. I had no choice but to go on.

I remember that the windows of the cab were down and the summer air blasting in was threatening rain. I knew I was treading at the lowest ebb of my life, a moment that was made only more surreal by the fact that my tuxedo was lying next to me in a garment bag and there was, at that very moment, a plane flying in from the east end of Long Island to take me back to a very important social function, over which I was expected to preside.

And so I was already in trajectory, and it was too late to cancel or postpone or go back, even though that's what I wanted to do. I've always loved being the auctioneer. I always enjoyed the certain amount of clamor that has serenaded my job. But how could I look forward to what lay ahead of me when there was someone I wanted to be with, a man I deeply loved who had very little time left?

What lay ahead was a benefit dinner/auction of fifty-six birdhouses, designed and donated by some of the most prominent architects in America: among others, Michael Graves, Robert Venturi, Charles Gwathmey, and Robert Stern. This was the first experiment in what would soon become a whole new territory of auctioneering: the emphemera of fantasy objects and privileges that would touch down into the world of acquisition just once and then vanish forever. For these objects there was no wholesale or retail, no comparative value. The prospective bidders were a gathering of well-heeled, well-known, well-intentioned guests, including many of New York's society luminaries, artists, celebrities, and successful businessmen, including Alfred Taubman, the owner of Sotheby's.

I arrived at La Guardia. I boarded the waiting plane and took off. We flew over cars sitting almost immobile on the Long Island Expressway; we flew over the shoals of Long Island Sound. I watched the patchwork of the suburbs slowly breaking away in favor of the fingers of rich agricultural Long Island, the soothing-looking squares of potato fields. Finally, the plane banked out over the Atlantic and descended into the East Hampton airport.

The event was being held in a beautiful white tent in the museum garden. The dinner tables were garlanded with flowers, and candles flickered in the steady ocean breeze that was pacifying the midsummer heat. Too drained from a day's work and life's crises to feel nervous or eager, I approached the podium between the main course and dessert. Cheerful patrons were diving into their mousses, looking up at me and wondering why I was shouting. Though up there on the podium, I felt as if I were still in that airplane.

Auctioning the first lot was a bit of a struggle. Most people weren't planning on buying anything. They saw the sale as an after-dinner treat, like a nice glass of sherry. The first birdhouse was a simple design estimated at $1,000–$1,500, which had been positioned to warm up the audience. I practically had to pull teeth to get somebody to buy it for $800. When the second birdhouse, designed by Jacquelin Robertson, came up, I happened to notice that there was a competition between Al Taubman and William Paley of CBS. But the two tycoons were bidding against each other without much moxie. I could feel myself breaking into a sweat.

"My boss, Al Taubman, is very interested in this birdhouse, Mr. Paley," I suddenly announced to the gathering. I didn't think about what I was saying; the words just tumbled out. "You're not going to let him get away with it, are you?"

A few people gasped at my sudden audacity. But there were also a few chuckles.

"Alfred," I said. "I believe that you have more money than Bill Paley does, don't you?"

Another gasp, but now people were putting down their spoons and turning their chairs around. There was a substantial ripple of laughter.

The bidding took off. Paley against Taubman. Because everyone knew who was bidding, the waiting period to see who would win his whimsy was charged. Both men could easily afford to pay $100,000 if they wanted to. Bill Paley won the birdhouse for $5,750 as a present for Annette de la Renta.

I ended up egging on the bidders for the rest of the auction. I knew so many of the people sitting there in the tent—

I had been to their dinner parties, I had sold objects to them at auction—it was easy to heckle them. At one point, John Jay Mortimer and his wife, Sanga, began unwittingly to bid on the same birdhouse. I said, "If you two would sit next to each other, you wouldn't cost yourselves so much money. John Jay, Sanga, come on now—discuss what you're doing ahead of time. I'm always happy to take your money. It's your bid, John Jay." At that moment I crossed over an invisible social line and reinvented myself as the auctioneer that everyone has come to know.

In my college yearbook, there's a smiling picture of me acting as an auctioneer of lost-and-found articles from the student center. An earlier photo shows me working the boardwalk at Atlantic City, where there was a little auction house next door to the frozen custard stand I managed as a summer job in 1961 and 1962. I was the auction house shill. I'd bid two bucks for a toaster and run away, crying, "I got a toaster, I got a toaster for two bucks." When the sale was over, I brought back the toaster and earned a dollar. That was how I began.

1. Origins

I was born on New Year's Day, 1944, in Pensacola, Florida, where my father was stationed in the navy. When I was two years old, we went north to Philadelphia, and then in 1948 my father was offered a job as choir director at the First Methodist Church in York, Pennsylvania. We moved west across the state and settled in a two-family house. When we arrived in York, there were barely seven people in the choir; today there are hundreds, often more than in the congregation. My father has just retired from the church; he'd been there nearly fifty years.

The population of greater York was around 100,000 at the time I grew up (today it is over 300,000). Barbells are made there, as are caskets and false teeth. Families who were involved with those industries tended to settle in North, West, and South York. East York, where we lived, was more upscale. We lived two blocks off the Lincoln Highway, Route 30 on the map, a well-known road that, in the thirties, had some stately houses built along it. Two blocks in, on a street perpendicular to Lincoln Highway called East Findlay, in our semidetached house, we lived at the edge of suburbia. This meant you could go to the end of East Findlay and get yourself in trouble by falling into a pig sty. York, Pennsylvania, like most of America, later got malled, and when it got malled, the town lost its center.

My parents met when they were in sixth grade and have been together for seventy-odd years since. They never had enough money to join a country club, but because my father was affiliated with the church, we knew lots of people who did belong to country clubs, and many invitations were extended to us. I remember wishing that such swanky venues of relaxation were more a regular part of my life, not just something that happened occasionally and at the whim of other people. I often fantasized about escaping my semidetached existence.

I was called "Percy" by my classmates because I always had opinions that were much grander than I deserved or more expensive than my family's financial status allowed. My mother used to tell me, "When you come into a room you're immediately supercilious." The first time she said this to me, I was too young to understand what she meant. And yet I suppose I was a snob—I still am—out of insecurity.

I envied people who were able to afford new cars every year or two. We kept our '47 Oldsmobile until 1958, by which time it had become so bedraggled that I could no longer bear to look at it. Appearances were important to me then. I wore gabardine slacks to the first baseball game I ever played. I was more upset by the big mark the baseball glove made on my pants than about not making it to first base. I wasn't an athlete, but I did well in school.

I learned to love art from my namesake, Robert Ewalt, my maternal grandfather, who lived to the ripe old age of ninety-four and was able to amass a modest but fine collection of paintings. Of all his paintings, my favorite is one by the so-called Pennsylvania Impressionist, Cullen Yates, which was completed in 1917; my grandfather bought it to commemorate my mother's birth. Throughout his life, he gave my parents many of his paintings, including a marshy landscape done by William Haseltine, one of the nineteenth-century Luminists. I always loved the picture, and years later I told my parents that I was not going to wait until they died to own it. Besides, with three brothers, there was no guarantee that I'd even end up with it. One autumn I suggested that they give it to me as a Christmas present; thus they could exonerate themselves from several years of holiday gift obligations and could subsequently hand me a Christmas bow each December 25. They finally gave me the painting fifteen years ago.

My grandfather spent most of his life working in the oil business, until, at the age of sixty, he took a job with Noreen, a company whose principal product was hair dye. It was during a Noreen sales convention in the fifties that I made my first trip to New York, along with my family and my grandparents.

The journey in those days was a bit more arduous than it is now. Driving to Lancaster, Pennsylvania, we took the train from there to Penn Station. I'll never forget the moment when the train veered away from the Jersey Turnpike and afforded a view of Manhattan. Captivated by the stony graph of the skyline, I felt a jittery anticipation in my stomach. From then on, I was in a state of awe: the monumental gigantism of Penn Station; the very la-di-da Statler Hilton across the street. My grandfather's nickname was "Parson," which fit his ascetic nature—he never smoke or drank. But he took us to places in Manhattan where we never dreamed he'd go: the Latin Quarter nightclub; several all-night bars. At one point during that first whirlwind visit, I bought a copy of the *New York Times* and took to walking around with it folded under my arm. My brother Steve said, "What do you think, you live here?"

"Maybe," I said.

I wanted to be not a tourist but the man who came to New York to get finished.

My best friend in high school, Scott Bickle, was the son of the minister at First Methodist Church, where my father was choir director. Scott and I decided to follow in the Methodist tradition, and we applied to a Methodist college, Drew University in New Jersey, only twenty-four miles west of New York City. And when Drew offered me a scholarship, that clinched it for me.

Nevertheless, to get by financially, I earned extra money by doing nonacademic work. And whereas my aristocratic attitude made everybody at Drew assume that I came from means, I actually cleaned toilets from two to four o'clock in the morning—I chose that ungodly hour to avoid anyone's seeing me do it.

One of Drew University's degree requirements was four semesters of gym. I kept putting it off and putting it off until my senior year, when I was the only upperclassman left on campus who hadn't fulfilled his gym requirement. Because I had spent my junior year in Washington, D.C., and in London, I was able to get away with taking gym for only two semesters. And I talked the gym coach into giving me the needed credits by horseback riding. I bought a bunch of tickets from a hack stable nearby and said in my grand way, "This is what I'll be doing for my exercise."

Unfortunately, the word got out that Woolley was riding, and then everybody at Drew wanted to go. So during my last semester, this privilege was rescinded, and I was told to find another compensatory activity. That turned out to be rugby.

I chose rugby only because I had this quixotic passion for a member of the rugby team. It was the first time in my life I ever played a contact sport. I remember I was puking five days before the first scrimmage; for me, the whole idea of physical harm was beyond imagining. I spent nearly the whole game avoiding getting anywhere near the ball. And then I was standing totally by myself, when the ball came lopping over and stopped right in front of me, like some kind of accusation. And so I was obliged to pick it up. I ran and got creamed by what seemed like a thousand people. The guy who tackled me said, "You know, Woolley, you'd do a lot better if you kept your eyes open when you run."

All throughout high school I had considered myself to be too fat, a bad body image that I carried with me right through college. I was naive with both sexes until I was nineteen. Although in my early twenties I had more sex with women, my first homosexual encounter completely unnerved me. I spent a good bit of time denying that this was what I wanted to do, although I knew it was.

During my senior year at college, I kept mounting a soapbox to tell everybody I knew that I was gay. I can now admit to a motivation in this: I wanted the men to whom I was confessing to sleep with me. There were nights, Saturday nights mostly, when I'd have too much to drink and wander into the woods, supposedly to commit suicide, yelling, "Come save me," to any number of my straight male friends. With thirty years hindsight, it sounds sophomoric, and yet occasionally it worked.

But back then I was still yearning. Within twenty-four miles of New York City, I hadn't yet gotten close enough. I still wanted to get out of my old life. Like so many people who have spent their childhood dreaming of leaving their small-town life behind, I wanted to come to New York and reinvent myself.

◖◐ ◑◗

When I graduated in June of 1965, without a prospect for a job in New York City, my political science professor at Drew gave me a recommendation. A New Jersey Republican named John H. Ewing had just retired from business and wanted to enter politics in very upscale Somerset County, where he made his home. He was running for the office of freeholder, a fancy name for the local county commissioner, and hired me to work as his campaign manager. I was paid $55 a week and lived in a fourth-floor garret of Ewing's manse.

Ewing moved in a world of moneyed people: his wife, Allison, was one of the aristocractic Pynes; his Somerset County neighbors were Charlie Englehard and Malcolm Forbes; the Douglas Dillons lived in Peapack Gladstone. My first exposure to egregious wealth was a coming-out party for Susan Englehard, which was held at Cragwood, Allison née Pyne Ewing's former family house. This sort of event, which is quite normal for me now, dazzled me when I was twenty-one.

Part of the reason why I jumped at the chance to work in politics had to do with my conflicting feelings of sexuality, which I thought might somehow be sublimated in this very public arena. I was also making a last stab at heterosexuality, in a relationship with a woman named Janet Jones, one of the most beautiful women at Drew University, who during our senior year had taken on the loss of my virginity as a sociological project. While I was living with the Ewings, Janet and I would make love in my garret room, often several times a day; and even though I found myself fantasizing about the man on the rugby team, all the coming-out parties and cotillions I attended roused in me the idea of an engagement. When I ultimately proposed to Janet, she very wisely said no. The alternative, she kindly explained, was that I could get unhappily married to her for a very short period of time.

Janet's just refusal of marriage made me start thinking solidly about what I truly wanted to be. As I saw it, I was at a crossroads. I could pursue a life in politics or try to get involved in something more creative. And when the election was over in November, I made my choice.

2. Graduate School

I've always said that my life was one great serendipity. My first job in New York City was at the Rolls-Royce of antique stores, A La Vieille Russie. I'd heard about the job from my Drew University friend Ward Landrigan. Ward was in the class ahead of me and had applied to Columbia for a graduate degree in art history. One day he came by my room at Drew to bemoan the fact that he had been rejected by Columbia. He happened to mention a job opening in the accounts payable department at Sotheby's. I encouraged him to apply for it; at least he'd be working around art if not with it. I made him keep calling until he was able to get an interview. Soon after he was given the job, somebody dropped dead in the jewelry department and he found himself a trainee.

It was at a jewelry course the following year that Ward happened to meet Peter Schaffer, whose father owned the venerated antique store A La Vieille Russie. Alexander Schaffer was looking for a trainee, and his son asked Ward if he wanted the position. Ward was content to stay where he was at Sotheby's but kindly suggested my name. Mr. and Mrs. Schaffer wanted to teach somebody to manage the New York store while their two sons took over the family's Paris operation on the Rue Royale. They wanted to find someone who knew nothing, a tabula rasa upon whom they could impress their ideas about dealing in their own brand of antiquities.

Alexander Schaffer was a Hungarian Jewish émigré, who had run an antique jewelry business before he came to the United States in the late 1920s. For many years after his arrival, he worked for Armand Hammer as an agent/buyer. On behalf of Hammer he had purchased many Fabergé imperial Easter eggs (some of which are now on display at the Museum of Fine Arts in Richmond, Virginia). In 1936, Alexander and his wife, Ray, opened the Schaffer Collection of Russian Imperial Treasures at Rockefeller Center; they and NBC were the first tenants within that complex of buildings. The Schaffers maintained their business until the early forties, when they bought A La Vieille Russie from Jacques Zolitnitsky in Paris and brought it to America, eventually opening the shop at Fifty-ninth Street and Fifth Avenue.

I was hired in the autumn of 1965, shortly after John H. Ewing won his bid for election.

I acquired knowledge quickly. Sweeping up, dusting, cleaning objects, taking them out of showcases and putting them back in—this was better than any knowledge I could have accumulated from books. Hanging from the ceiling in the center of the store was a Russian chandelier of the Louis XVI period, whose panes of deep cobalt glass gave it a typically Russian-looking flair. Because I took down every piece of that chandelier and cleaned it, I came to learn exactly what I was handling. I learned how the pieces fit together, I discerned how it was made, and I felt as though I gleaned a sense, at least, of the inspiration that went into making it. Not that there weren't books available to read and time to read them. In a store such as A La Vieille Russie, which is probably one among a half dozen of the finest antique shops in the world, people are so intimidated by the prices and the contents that in fact the place isn't usually busy. And the Schaffers did not mind if I sat downstairs minding the shop, reading a book on French furniture if there was nothing else to do.

Halfway back in the store, a staircase makes a dramatic diagonal rise up to a balcony. It's the sort of staircase you see Hollywood divas descend in the movies. Very *Sunset Boulevard*. And indeed, while I sat at a desk below the balcony, a lot of celebrated people traipsed up those stairs to the inner sanctum where the Schaffers have their offices. Men like Gianni Agnelli and Stavros Niarchos would be immediately escorted upstairs by one of the Schaffers, to be shown the "pushy" objects—a Fabergé imperial egg or a Potsdam snuffbox— things that were considered too precious to be kept downstairs. But I found almost immediately that I had a knack for selling the less expensive inventory, like cuff links and antique jewelry. Soon it became a small joke in the store that almost nobody could come in and see me without spending some money. When customers revealed their fears that the things we sold would be too expensive, I would say to them, "Well, nothing in this shop is expensive. We just happen to have a lot of things that cost a lot of money." And they were often pleasantly surprised.

For example, we used to stock Karelian birch-root cigarette cases that we imported from the Soviet Union. Then we had gold double-headed eagles, the Romanov crest, cast down on Forty-seventh Street in the jewelry district. It was my job to scratch the surface of the case, lace the markings I made with glue, and affix the double-headed eagle, transforming the cigarette case into something that looked pre-Revolutionary.* I remember an incomplete set of fruit knives with bloodstone handles and gilded blades that I turned into letter openers and sold one at a time.

One rainy Saturday afternoon, an austere-looking lady wearing a trench coat arrived at the store. Her hair was visibly mussed from the weather. She said, "I'd like to see some of your little Fabergé things." So we went under the balcony to the display case, and something immediately struck her eye. "What's that?" she said. "That's very pretty."

I checked the tag and informed her: "This is a gold-mounted leaf-form carved bloodstone bonbonnière made in Saint Petersburg in 1905." She said, "How much is it?" and I said, "Three thousand eight hundred dollars." She said, "I'll have it."

No human being had ever spoken to me so frivolously about such a large sum of money. I owed the government $3,800 for college. Until this point, my most pricey sale at A La Vieille Russie had been a pair of $400 cuff links.

I was unnerved by the woman's self-assurance. I tried to collect myself as I sat her down at a little table at the bottom of the stairs. I said, "May I have your name, please."

"Mrs. Paul Mellon," she said.

"One or two *l*'s?"

"Two," she said.

"And your address, please?"

"One twenty-five East Seventieth."

"Apartment number."

"Well, it's actually a house," she said diffidently.

---

*Our prospective customers were always informed that these cigarette cases were homespun souvenirs.

I certainly wasn't going to hand such a precious object over to a stranger. "Can I deliver this for you?"

"No," she said, looking at me directly. "I'd actually like to take it with me right now."

I asked if she had an account with us; I don't think Mrs. Mellon had been asked that question for quite a while. She hesitated a bit. Which made me suspicious. "May I see your driver's license?"

She looked at me shrewdly and was actually getting out her wallet when Mr. Schaffer came downstairs, recognized her, and took over in a hurry. After that, nevertheless, Bunny Mellon would ask for me whenever she came into the shop.

On another occasion, Charlotte Ford came in to find something for her sister Anne's wedding to an Uzielli. At the time, I didn't know who Charlotte Ford was. I remember how she said, "My sister is getting married very soon. And I need a little prezzy for the wedding. Nothing too expensive. About one or two thou." When you come from a small town in Pennsylvania, sentences like that just don't happen. And in 1965, when you could buy large apartments for $10,000, that was serious money, although, I suppose, for a Ford not a whole lot to spend on your sister's wedding present. Charlotte picked out a Fabergé-like bird on a perch.

One afternoon, when I was in the midst of lining the store window with a lot of porcelain plates with the Romanov double-headed eagle, Gianni Agnelli happened to pass by. The moment he came inside, I recognized him as one of the people who'd already paraded up the stairs to the Schaffers' inner sanctum. "Do you have any more of these plates?" he asked me.

A bit more confident now, I nearly said, "That's like asking

Chrysler if they sell Dodges." But I knew the reference would be lost on him, and in those days I was still bending over backward to be polite. I told him we had lots. Virtually all the porcelain we owned had been made in the Imperial Porcelain Factory that was founded by Empress Elizabeth in 1744, and it most often came with that Romanov double-eagle crest.

He said, "I'll have them all."

That, too, was not something you heard in York, Pennsylvania, but I was becoming professionally blasé.

I spent the rest of that afternoon searching every cabinet, every cupboard, every shelf, for every plate with a double-headed eagle, all of which were then sent on to Agnelli's home in Turin. These plates were worth between one and two hundred dollars in 1965, certainly cheaper than new plates at Tiffany's. But the Romanov plates are still valuable now as antiques, whereas modern plates are worth maybe 10 percent of their value the day after they are bought.

Still, because this was A La Vieille Russie, we were able to sell many things on the name of the store alone. *Provenance* is a French word that is used to describe this: how much potential buyers want to overpay for something that either belongs to a venerable gallery, shop, or institution, or belongs to someone a lot more famous than they are. We had a desk set made by the English silversmith Vickers and Company, a very elaborate, over-the-top, Louis XV rococo-style silver-mounted tortoiseshell desk set. Blotter, pen, mirror—all of it bearing the monogram of the empress Alexandra, the last czarina, the wife of Nicholas II. The blotter had the czarina's signature in facsimile reverse, which meant she actually used it. The Schaffers were able to buy the desk set very reasonably. It wasn't terribly antique, or terribly pretty; I had always found tortoiseshell more difficult to sell than plain veneer. After writing a full description of the set, I approached Alexander Schaffer and asked him what we should mark as the price.

Without hesitation, he said, "Put twenty-eight thousand dollars on it."

In those years, as the result of my firm Methodist upbringing, I was of the mind that whatever you paid for something, you mark it up at the most 100 percent. And because I had a blank, perhaps disapproving look on my face, Mr. Schaffer said to me, "I want to ask you something, Robert: What corner are we on?"

"Fifty-ninth and Fifth," I said.

"And isn't it the most expensive retail corner in New York City?"

I agreed that it probably was.

He said, "Now, I've been in the business for over sixty years. Is it worth something, my expertise?"

"Oh, certainly, Mr. Schaffer," I said.

"So, as I was saying, mark it twenty-eight thousand dollars."

I did what he said, but I thought: This ugly desk set will never sell at that price.

Mr. Schaffer, as often happens in Jewish families, was much easier on me than on his sons. I was allowed to ask him stupid questions once. Whereas if either Peter or Paul asked a stupid question of their father, they'd be excoriated. Needless to say, when I first went to work at A La Vieille Russie, neither son was thrilled. Paul, because he was the firstborn, was always put under a lot of pressure and was ambivalent about me. Peter was basically ignored, left to fend for himself; and it would stand to reason that in light of this, he was not very tolerant of my stupidities. Nevertheless, both sons were keenly made to realize that knowledge of Russian art is something that cannot be inherited but must be carefully acquired.

A month and a half after my exchange with Mr. Schaffer, King Hassan of Morocco turned up in the store. All royalty, I have learned, behave more or less uniformly. They always travel with a "Major Domo," who follows them around the store, taking notes as they say, "I find this interesting, I find that interesting." Then the entourage leaves. The next day, Major Domo returns and starts negotiating fiercely on a whole bunch of items. As it turned out, King Hassan was smitten with the desk set, and his majordomo began bargaining for it. Especially because the king was bidding on so many things, we had lots of room to negotiate. After all, the king has to think he's getting a deal, so he demands a discount. Though the Schaffers may have indicated differently to this majordomo, it was hardly a burden on them to knock 20 percent off the entire purchase.

Then again, many customers were not as decisive as King Hassan. I remember one wealthy woman coming in for months and months, looking at a certain French commode.* It was in pristine condition, a perfectly preserved rarity that was priced at almost $30,000, which admittedly was a good deal of money back in the late sixties. And yet I felt sure this woman could afford it, because she kept coming in to moon over it, wearing an array of Chanel suits, silk dresses, and fur coats. She said to me, "This is very expensive." And I said my line: "No, no, nothing's expensive. We just have a lot of things that cost a lot of money." Although I have found that nuance quite useful over the years, it clearly was not working with this prospective client.

Some weeks after our conversation, the commode sold to a regular patron of the store, who bought it without even a hes-

*When I first arrived at A La Vieille Russie, I thought a commode was anything but a chest of drawers.

itation. And one day after it was gone, the woman bustled into the store, saw that it was gone, and turned to me, flabbergasted. "Where's my commode?" she demanded.

I gave her a frosty stare and said, "I don't understand that pronoun."

"What happened to my commode?"

I had grown tired of her coming into the shop and ogling something that she could have easily afforded. "*Your* commode?" I repeated. "Unless you bought it and actually took it away, it's not yours."

In the trade, as it were, the difference between the shop and the auction is that the auction process focuses the mind. If the same commode had come up for bidding, she would've had to make up her mind in an instant, and perhaps she would have had to pay even more than $30,000 for it.

As time went on, I dealt more and more with Russian enamelwork. The Schaffers carried quite a lot of it, but it wasn't their taste. They thought it déclassé. Fair enough. I got to know the enamelwork because I spent so much time cleaning it. Most of the enamel we carried was made between 1880 and World War I. I was partial to a very opulent kind of Byzantine cloisonné, its blend of gold-plated filigree and enamel considered less expensive than something that was wholly enameled, which involved a costly and time-consuming process. While at A La Vieille Russie, I made the decision that "shaded enamels" should be more expensive than those of more standard colors. Shaded enamels were variations that were more difficult to achieve in the kiln and therefore more costly.

Many of the major Russian enamel dealers of today bought their initial pieces from me at A La Vieille Russie: Leo Kaplan began his collecting when he was still in the lumber business;

Harry Kraut, to whom I sold his first enameled spoon, now, hundreds of thousands of dollars later, has an enormous collection of Russian enamelware, part of which he has been selling recently at Sotheby's.

I had a knack for divining what people desired, perhaps because my life at the time was fraught with unfulfilled desire. I was still conflicted about my sexuality. Throughout my twenties, I tried to exorcise these conflicts in heavy drinking. And the more I drank, the more uninteresting and unattractive I felt I became. I found myself pursuing straight men, because I figured they were as unattainable as I was unattractive. It was a pretty dismal equation.

From the age of twenty-one until I was twenty-eight and suffered a severe bout of hepatitis B, I spent most of my evenings in straight bars, drinking, and put on at least ten pounds a year. I began every evening with Courvoisier on the rocks at six o'clock. Frequently, after I got home, I'd induce a few hours of sleep with a drink or so and then, at 11:00 P.M. or midnight, go out to a bar called Mike Malkan's, which was the second singles bar in the world, after Friday's. I'd stay at Malkan's until I closed it at four in the morning, at which point I'd continue on to an after-hours place. Often I went directly from whatever after-hours establishment I was currently patronizing to A La Vieille Russie. Although I had had no sleep whatsoever, I'd at least sobered up by the time I was due at work. The Schaffers, as far as I knew, never had any idea of what I was up to.

Then, in 1968, I received a draft notice. I was in therapy at the time, and my psychiatrist wrote a letter for me that read: "Robert Woolley has deep interpersonal relationship problems culminating in overt homosexual activity." As recently as the late 1960s, it must be remembered, homosexuality was still thought of as a mental illness that was curable. Taking that letter with me to the army induction office down on Whitehall Street, I wore a three-piece Brooks Brothers suit, held an umbrella, and carried a *New York Times* under my arm, a *New York Times* whose headlines were devoted to the raging Tet offensive. And when the army recruiter read the letter, he looked me up and down and said, "Really?" He seemed to have trouble believing my letter, because I didn't meet his preconceived notions of "fluffy." But once I soberly assured him the letter was accurate, he drew a pink heart on my clipboard and wrote: "Room 286." Then I was given an eye exam and an intelligence test and waited around until the announcement: "Anybody with Room 286, please proceed."

Room 286 was filled with people who either were too stupid to have passed the no-brainer intelligence test or were wearing fluffy sweaters—other homosexuals. We were to be interviewed by a psychiatrist. And when it was my turn to be seen, I said to him, "If you want to put me in some corps that loves the enemy to death, I'd be thrilled. But if it's a matter that you might not want me because I'm a homosexual, then you'd better not have me." They agreed not to have me, and I was through with the threat of Vietnam and the United States Army by 10:30 A.M. After watching several movies on Forty-second Street, I showed up at A La Vieille Russie at around four-thirty and announced: "The X ray of that old rugby injury worked fine. I'm still yours."

The Schaffers were relieved to hold on to me. They knew that I had a knack for selling. By then I had moved quickly beyond selling expensive curios; I had developed a special empathy for the Russian icon. Perhaps these Orthodox religious images were more deeply branded in me because of my Sunday school background. Who would've thought that going to church would prepare me for the secular vocation of selling icons.

Even though I didn't know the story of each one, I could easily divine the theology behind what was in the picture. Many times people bought icons because of their own names. A man named Andrew might be drawn to an icon of Saint Andrew. Or if somebody was about to go to a religious ceremony, a wedding, a baptism, it would be quite easy for me to pick an icon that would fit the occasion.

In 1967, two years after I began working at A La Vieille Russie, the Helena Rubinstein estate was sold at Sotheby Parke Bernet. I had gone to a few minor auctions as a representative of the Schaffers and bid as their proxy; since they were well known, they often preferred to be discreet in their bidding. They sent me over to Sotheby Parke Bernet during the "decorations" viewing of the Rubinstein sale, to look at her collection of icons. These icons had not been separated out for the special collectors but were mixed in with many other decorative objects as part of the larger estate sale. In those days, the auction house tried harder to keep an estate intact rather than dismantle it and sell the important art in its appropriate category.

Nevertheless, these Rubinstein icons were probably the best collection on the market during my lifetime. In the sale catalog, Sotheby's chose to illustrate a silver-covered enamel icon of Saint Nicholas. It was not a very exciting example—nineteenth-century, a bit common. But there were ten superb, well-documented fourteenth- and fifteenth-century icons that had been undercataloged and not illustrated. One, called *The Three Marys,* was truly extraordinary. The Schaffers had authorized me to bid on it and all the others. It was my first major dealing with Sotheby's and one of the few occasions when I faced the great auction house from the buyer's side. What an incredible thrill it was to have so little competition for the lots and to buy everything I was supposed to bid on for under $30,000. The Schaffers had cleared me to bid a great deal more.

The icons ended up being sleepers. In the trade, a "sleeper" is something that only the cognoscenti recognize, an object worth lots of money that one is able to buy for relatively little. The day after I collected the icons, the Schaffers sold one of them for $50,000. Ultimately, however, they decided that most of these icons would be more profitable as long-term investments and decided to hang on to them. Today I believe they would refuse a million dollars for *The Three Marys.*

3. A Rainy Day

Parke-Bernet, the oldest auction house in America, had its origins in a New York City gallery called the American Art Association. Founded in 1883, the American Art Association merged with the Anderson Gallery, a New York auction house, at the end of the nineteenth century and thereafter inauspiciously called itself the American Art Association Anderson Galleries, or AAAAG. When the company began to founder during the Depression of the mid-1930s, it was bought out by two of its principals, Hiram Parke and Otto Bernet (pronounced Burnette; a Swiss German, Otto Bernet hated the idea of being Frenchified). The Parke-Bernet Gallery was formed in 1936 and established itself in the Bergdorf Building, in the space that is now occupied by Van Cleef & Arpels.

Parke-Bernet remained in the Bergdorf Building until the late 1940s, when it was contacted by Robert Dowling, who owned a company named City Investing. Dowling was a progressive financier who had wanted to encourage business in the zones above Fifty-seventh Street (during those years, Madison Avenue north of Seventieth Street was considered an outlying area). Dowling first bought the Carlyle Hotel, in the early forties, then set his sights on the land across the street, which was occupied by a greenhouse. There he built an office space that looked like a polished limestone sugar cube, an architecturally nondescript building whose reigning feature was a cast-aluminum frieze of a woman in gossamer garments towering over a half-naked youth. Designed by the sculptor Wheeler Williams, the frieze was called *Venus Seducing Manhattan*. And in 1948 Bob Dowling seduced Parke-Bernet uptown to his new limestone building.

These days it's hard to imagine an auction house purposely limiting its business and still surviving, and yet this is precisely how Parke-Bernet operated until 1964, when it was bought by Sotheby's. For a stipulation in Dowling's lease stated that if the gallery's gross receipts exceeded $9 million per year, the rent would rise steeply. As a result, certain private deals were made by the auction house that were not written down in the books, which Dowling reviewed.

Then again, throughout the nineteenth century and the first half of the twentieth, art auctions were much more leisurely. Unlike its counterparts in London, Sotheby's and Christie's, Parke-Bernet, though it had experts in various fields, did not have any specialized departments. More often than not, auctions were a potpourri of linens and lace, rugs, glassware, porcelain, some paintings, and a few pieces of furniture. An auction was more a social event than anything else. No important collector considered selling a significant picture at an auction; indeed, the idea of selling one's favorite collectibles to the highest bidder was considered rather bourgeois. Fierce competition was unheard of, except in the matter of getting a table for lunch across the street at the Carlyle, which was the custom of many people before they attended Parke-Bernet's afternoon sales.

Sotheby's, meanwhile, had flourished in England for two centuries before its arrival in America. Its first sale, on March 12, 1744, in London, brought in £876 for a consignment of books. (In those days, one or two pounds could pay the yearly wages of an upstairs maid.) Until the 1920s, Sotheby's auctioned only books. Christie's, which has been around almost as long, dealt in household furnishings, art, and other collectibles.

In 1960, Peter Wilson, the chairman of Sotheby's, established a permanent New York office, which was managed by Peregrine Pollen, a well-born Briton who was a charming, charismatic businessman. Pollen was able to scare up a great deal of patronage from American art collectors, convincing them they would get higher prices for their consignments in London-based auctions. In this way, Parke-Bernet began losing more and more business to Sotheby's, and when Parke-Bernet's CEO, Leslie Hyam, died in 1963, the shareholders of the company began considering the idea of selling. Wilson, in the meantime, had begun pushing for the acquisition of Parke-Bernet; and when he decided to buy the company for $1 million, his fellow directors were so flabbergasted by what they felt was an exorbitant sum that half of them resigned. In an era when American companies were snapping up English companies left and right, it was something of a reversal of trends for an English firm to buy an American one. But Wilson believed that there were people with a lot of money in America, people who wanted and had the resources to acquire art.

Most of the staff at Parke-Bernet were incorporated into the hybrid company, including Louis Marion, Parke-Bernet's principal auctioneer, as well as his son John. A year after the merger, Louis Marion left to pursue his own interests in the art world, whereas his son stayed on with the understanding that once Peregrine Pollen returned to London, John Marion would inherit the mantle of the presidency of the company.

Shortly after the Helena Rubinstein sales in 1967, Ward Landrigan tipped me off about a position at Sotheby's as an assistant in the furniture department. Ward managed to secure me an interview with Marcus Linell, head of decorative arts, and Peter Wilson, who was in America at the time. When I met them, they were impressed by the fact that I had apprenticed with an old established antique firm such as A La Vieille Russie. I seemed young and eager to learn, and so they offered me the job.

The news of my potential hiring reached John Marion, who was then a vice president. John remembered having seen me raving drunk at a Long Island party given by Ward Landrigan. A woman friend of mine (who happened to be sleeping with one of Sotheby's board members) informed me that John had gone to Marcus and Peter and told them that he thought I was too unstable to work in the art auction business. What he didn't realize then is that you *must* be psychologically unstable to work in this world.

And so Marcus Linell unhired me one rainy evening in front of the Parke-Bernet Galleries. He didn't give me a concrete reason, but I knew why. As I was on my way to make dinner at Ward and Judith Landrigan's, I had come to the final interview holding two bags of groceries. No sooner did I hear the disappointing news than I said my good-byes and dashed across the street to the Carlyle, where there were several purring limousines. Marcus watched as in my purposeful fury I bribed a driver with ten dollars and then jumped in the car to be whisked away. He told me later that my stylish getaway struck a chord in him. On pure hunch, he went back to the board of Sotheby's and told them he'd take full responsibility for hiring me.

Once I was rehired, I went to lunch with Peregrine Pollen, who was then the president of Sotheby's North America, Peter Wilson, and Marcus Linell. Wilson said to me, "Well, Robert, you've worked in one of the finest places in the world. Now I'm afraid you're going to be disappointed, because we sell a lot of junk, even if I spell it with a *q-u-e*."

"No," I responded. "I want to work here." Then I said, "I know a lot about Russian works of art."

"That's all well and good," Wilson said, "but since you're being hired to work in the furniture department, we're anxious for you to learn about furniture."

Peregrine Pollen added, "And don't expect to come and work for Sotheby's in order to make a lot of money. You should be coming to Sotheby's because of your passion for what you'll be selling."

Nevertheless, I got their attention by telling them what had happened at the Helena Rubinstein sale. "You don't quite realize that the finest collection of icons that has ever been on the market, which my former employers now own, were so grossly undercataloged that it would seem they were done by somebody who said, 'It's an icon, it's square.' " I took an appropriate pause, registering the shocked faces at my table. "This must never happen again. And let me show how it won't happen again." I brandished the Helena Rubinstein catalog and went through the icons one by one, telling them how much I'd paid for each of them and letting them know that I'd acquired *The Three Marys* for only $850. The problem, I explained, was that the icons had been thrown into the middle of a sale of apartment decorations. Sotheby's had thought they had done quite well with the Rubinstein sale. Certainly there had been many wonderful objects and paintings. And Rubinstein's name, her provenance, had inspired furious bidding on certain lots. But this situation gave me the ammunition to tell them just how much they had not earned.

I pointed out that the top icon dealers in Europe had obviously not received the catalog because it was a furniture catalog. I told them there was a London dealer named Dick Temple, who, had he known about the auction, would have forced me to bid my entire bidding allowance. There I was at twenty-four years old, telling Marcus Linell, the head of decorative arts, and Peter Wilson, the chairman, how to do business. I suggested that a better way to market the Russian art would be to hold at least two yearly sales of pieces deliberately pulled from estate offerings: one in December, the other in June. The three men just sat there, gaping at me. Finally, they told me to continue learning about furniture but to proceed with cataloging Russian works of art for an imminent sale.

This was a new direction for the company. Until now, there had been sales in jewelry and furniture and paintings, but nothing so specific in New York as a national art category, though London had many such sales.

⟪◉ ◉⟫

And so, almost immediately, I began working toward a sale of Russian art, which I approached with a mixture of complete ignorance and good sense. I went around to all the departments at Sotheby's, identifying Russian objects and pulling them out. I siphoned Russian porcelain from the porcelain department, I collected Russian silver from the silver department, I combed for enamel from decorative arts and nabbed a few paintings from fine arts. Needless to say, the department heads were irritated by me. I contacted all the dealers with whom I'd done business at A La Vieille Russie and culled as much as I could from private sources whom I'd met along the way. I knew how to identify the objects, but obviously I had to learn Sotheby Parke-Bernet's special way of cataloging them.

I remember one day during that period when I found Marcus Linell sitting behind a whole tableful of Russian enamelware. He hadn't an idea of what any of it was. "This is a shaded enamel *kovsh*," I said, picking up a boat-shaped drinking vessel. "Made by Pavel Ovchinikov, a contemporary of Fabergé, probably around 1900. But it's black with tarnish. We can't sell it like this. We won't get anything for it. We have to clean it."

At A La Vieille Russie I had learned how to clean everything and put it in smart retail shape. But they were not used to doing this at Sotheby's; rather, they left most of their decorative inventory in the "as is" condition. I told Marcus about something called Instant Dip, which worked beautifully if used judiciously. The danger was that if you didn't immediately rinse off the cleaner, some of the weaker or lighter gilding on the enamelwork could also "instant dip" away.

In the meantime, I kept nudging John Marion, our chief auctioneer (whose opinion of me had changed quite dramatically during my first three months): "I want to make my debut at my debut." It was unheard of for a newcomer like me to begin auctioning anything of value. After being trained and observing the "masters" at work, one was expected to begin with book auctions where articles were sold for ten or twelve dollars. But I was very pushy, and they agreed to let me auctioneer my Russian sale.

John and I would sit in his office, and he would create the scenario of an auction and fire questions at me about reserve, price, and bidder and then try to trip me up. It was a training method that had been initiated by his father. What I basically learned through John Marion and through my own trial and error distills down to three virtues of auctioneering: consistency, control, and communication.

Consistency refers to one's style of gaveling the lots. You cannot bring the hammer down quickly on one lot and then take more time on the next. For one thing, it drives people crazy, but for another, it leaves you wide open for the complaint that you didn't acknowledge a bidder in the back of the room. One of the first things John Marion told me was that I always had to be one step ahead of the room: to develop an instinct, to read what's going on, to smell out the serious bidders as opposed to the more skittish ones, who are jumping in and out and who tend to drop out of the race long before it ends.

It always helps to know who is in the audience. Before doing an auction, John Marion used to go through the catalog with the heads of the various departments involved in the sale and familiarize himself with who might be bidding on the more pricey lots. Learning, for example, that X and Y dealers had expressed interest in a certain Gauguin, he would remind himself in his auctioneer's book to look at those persons when the lot came up.

The style I developed was to learn the behavior nuances of regular clients. Over the years, one collector who used to buy at Sotheby's would always get upset when, anticipating her bid, I would look at her, waiting for her to enter the fray. I knew her taste, what she was going to be bidding on. Finally, I told her, "You think you're very clever because you don't betray any emotion. But three to six lots ahead of whatever you're interested in, your shoulders go back and you start shuffling your feet, and so I'm on to you." This woman was once a well-known surgeon in Boston, who fit my cliché for surgeons: "They cut three days a week and collect the other two." She has since retired from her medical practice and become a jewelry dealer. She had one of the great collections of French furniture, until we sold it for her.

You always have to make it clear who has the bid, where it is, and how much it is. For example, "It's the lady's bid, front left, at ten thousand dollars." If I say that, then anybody else who thinks it might be his bid knows it can't be. Now, obviously, at certain times, you are going to have a lot of people waving at you, and the key is always to deal with only two bidders at a time. If you have two people standing next to each other and bidding, you have to choose one of them to compete with whatever other bid you have. You have to spot confusion and clear it up immediately: "I'm sorry, sir, it's the lady's bid to the left of you." The people who help you keep track of the audience are called "bid spotters." Dressed in their dark blue jackets and dark slacks, they stand at the front and on the sides of the salesroom and are the extra eyes and ears of the auctioneer. Bid spotters are part of the company's union staff, Teamsters who are also responsible for any physical moving of the art and objects throughout the company and to and from exhibitions and private residences.

During an auction, the auctioneer must always give priority to the "order bids" placed by interested clients in advance of the sale at the Bids Office. Their names are written down in the "auctioneer's book," the catalog the auctioneer keeps referring to while he or she is up on the podium. Because most auctions take place in the morning and afternoon, many people have difficulty attending them, because of work or other commitments, and a vast majority leave bids. People who place order bids usually have an account at Sotheby's. They'll call up and authorize us to bid up to, say, $10,000 for a certain thing. A good auctioneer treats his book not only as a human being but as a dear friend. So even if there are twenty hands up for a lot, I will pick two—the book and somebody in the room. I will never accept a bid in the room that is equal to one in the order book. If the lot begins with a bid of $5,000 and someone has authorized bidding up to $10,000, then I'll keep referring to the book to bid against the room until the book is satisfied. And once the book is satisfied, then I will look for the second bidder, either on the phone or in the room itself.

The room naturally gains an advantage over one of our bids personnel who are working the phones. Our bids staff speak many different languages, and often during an auction they are called upon to translate from one language to another and back—as well as to multiply and convert different currencies mentally (although nowadays the mathematical calculations for each currency are done by computer and, as the bidding increases, digitally displayed on a board above the stage in the salesroom). Often, by the time the bids personnel have spoken to their clients abroad, I've traveled way past the price. I try to lighten up and wait if I can, but that can be irritating to the people in the room who are bidding promptly.

At auctions there is often someone in the back who is waving his hand at me as though I'm totally ignoring him. "I'm bidding! I'm bidding!" he shouts. But what difference does it make if I'm acknowledging him or somebody in the front row?

The point is that the price is climbing, and when it slows its ascent the person in the back of the room will have plenty of time to spend his money. To get him to stop fussing, I usually have to say, "Sir [or Madam], I will get to you when I finish with these two." And I've learned to throw in, "if you have any money left," in the case of an obnoxious person. Ninety-nine times out of a hundred, the loud party in the back has dropped conspicuously out of view by the time it really counts.

There were so many things I was trying to remember that morning of my first sale, as I spoke to friends and rang up key dealers and reminded them to come. I was wonderfully nervous. I thought I would know most of the people in the room: collectors I'd dealt with over the last three years, even my old bosses, the Schaffers. Some of the dealers had already given me good-natured flak because I'd had everything cleaned, especially the Russian enamelwork that was blackened with age. They kept telling me I was using pristine condition as a reason to raise the estimates.

I remember the salesroom felt warm the moment I walked in, and my cheeks felt it more than any other part of my body. I scanned the crowd and registered that two hundred people had clustered in a gallery that could easily hold a thousand. But the place felt packed. I climbed up onto what we call the "preacher's podium," a hexagonal dais, and just before I began, I felt a strange calm come over me. I felt comfortable up there. I knew that it was where I was supposed to be.

"Ladies and gentlemen, we have for your competition today a sale of Russian works of art. I call your attention to the

Conditions of Sale in the catalog." And off I went. The first object that I auctioned was an icon of Saint Nicholas of Mojaisk of the eighteenth century, which was rolled out on the stage beside me. A twittering went through the crowd. I sold through fifty lots of objects in just under an hour.

4. Making My Way

My first sale was a success. And in each sale I did thereafter, Sotheby Parke Bernet made more and more money. Soon the Russian sales were bringing in more than a million dollars, then more than two million. Today such sales in Russian art can bring upwards of five million dollars annually. The return climbs a lot higher if there are Fabergé imperial eggs involved. Fabergé eggs alone have brought as much as five or six million dollars each.

Even today many Americans think an auction is something along the lines of a cattle sale, where the auctioneer is muttering nearly incomprehensibly. And in fact, many of these auctioneers work for firms that actually own the merchandise they're auctioning. This method of selling is called "advanced bid auctioning." If someone leaves a bid of $2,000, it's going to cost $2,000, even if the room falls asleep or there's a blizzard and nobody shows up. Many auctioneers sell each lot at high speed to drive up a price as high as possible. If, for example, during an advanced bid auction, someone raises a hand to bid $9,000, often the auctioneer will clock him in at

$10,000, and before the bidder knows it, the price has risen to $11,000 and he feels as if he's bidding against himself.

It's quite different at Sotheby's. We don't own the merchandise; we just present it in the most favorable light: inform the prospective buyer about its historical context and guarantee its authenticity. Whenever I'm auctioneering and anything is sold, I always write down the location and number of the underbidder so that if a buyer accuses me of pushing him up to a certain amount, I have the comfort of telling him that if he really doesn't want what he bought, I know how to get in touch with the person who bid slightly less.

Even though advanced bid auctioning is not something that is done at Sotheby's, people are still wary and feel as though they have to know somebody to know what's going on. With vague memories of slapstick comedy, people have been known to ask, "If I scratch my nose, do I own it?" And I say, "If you scratch your nose or you wave to a friend in the back of the auction gallery, perhaps I will embarrass you by calling a bid because I love doing it." But I will proceed in a straightforward, cautious manner. Rarely do people bid for things unintentionally. Certainly there have been genuine mistakes, but usually we know the person who makes them and are able to rectify the matter if it is handled promptly.

Before 1974, one thing that auction houses had going against them was *caveat emptor,* or "buyer beware." The catalogs stated that we were selling in "as is" condition, which basically gave us the right to lie, cheat, and steal. We avoided doing this for obvious ethical business reasons. We need to be reputable, relied upon; if, for example, we learned that we'd sold a fake, we'd give back the buyer's money; if something was overcataloged, we made adjustments. Still, you couldn't quite convince buyers 100 percent. In the old Conditions of Sale, the seed of doubt had been planted before the auction even began.

Finally, I said to my colleagues at Sotheby's, "We act as if we have a guarantee; why don't we just get rid of *caveat emptor?* Then we'll have a great marketing strategy." For people in the trade—dealers, designers, and decorators—had been using our "buyer beware" clause to ward off the general public. Which is why during the sixties and seventies only 20 percent of our business was with individual collectors and 80 percent was with the trade.

And yet having other people bid for the same lot, people who are willing to pay, say, $95,000 for something that you buy for $100,000, can be comforting. Whereas spending $100,000 for something with a private dealer can give an overwhelming feeling that the object may have been marked up two and a half times and should be negotiable. This is why our business is now 70 percent individuals and 30 percent trade. It's also the main reason why our gross sales have risen from $17 million in New York in 1968 to a high of over $1.5 billion in 1989. Today an average good year brings in between $500 million and $1 billion. With a few legal stipulations, there is now a guarantee of authenticity. Now it's *in print* that if somebody buys something at Sotheby's and finds out within five years that it's a fake, he gets his money back. Anything we can do to allay the fears of the consumer we'll do.

The irony is that not much that is stolen comes up at auction, because an auction is so public. Once, I remember, a pair of tapestries in a catalog just happened to be sent to the palazzo of the man in Italy from whom they had been stolen. He was able to send us photographs of the tapestries in his salon. In such a case, because we don't own the disputed object, we have to tell the consignor that the title is not clear, that somebody else claims ownership, and that it has to be sorted out by lawyers before we'll relinquish it to anyone.

Famously, a Chagall was stolen from the Guggenheim Museum years ago. The painting went into the so-called trade and was purchased, nearly twenty years after its disappearance. The Guggenheim did not report the theft. And the purchaser, a woman collector, claimed that if they weren't interested in finding the painting enough to report its disappearance, she should rightfully get to keep it. Just so. But the law states that once anything is stolen it remains stolen property and the title cannot pass. The woman was paid good money for her troubles and the painting went back to the museum.

Although the category of Russian works of art proved a viable one for Sotheby's, it didn't mean that everything Russian that subsequently came in was automatically hived off and put in the Russian sales. In fact, even today there can be a dilemma when we feel an estate of somebody not that well known ought to be kept together. When you're not dealing with such obvious draws as the Duchess of Windsor or Elton John, an estate kept intact will often create more of a buzz. But if such an estate contains a fair amount of Russian art, we make sure to send the catalog to the people who we know subscribe to Russian works of art. The best situation, of course, is to try to keep an estate sale together and siphon off some of the more important work for a forthcoming sale in its appropriate category. In another words, having your cake and eating it.

At the age of twenty-five, I was already considered something of a whippersnapper. When I got wind that Marcus Linell and Peregrine Pollen were going to Russia to "shop," I said, "Why are you two going? Neither of you knows anything about this stuff. And if you're going to give advice about buying it, you'd better have somebody along who can differentiate the seventeenth century from the nineteenth and know what everything is worth." Perhaps taken aback by my forthrightness, they agreed.

In 1969, the cold war was still on, and the only real way to get anything out of the Soviet Union was to buy it through the Satra Corporation, an American company that dealt in minerals and bought huge amounts of chromium ore from the Russians. Satra was owned by an Armenian who spoke Russian and did tens of millions of dollars' worth of business. One of Satra's high-ranking executives, John Kapstein, had got in touch with Sotheby's. He told us that by using Satra as a middleman, we could buy Russian works of art from Novo-Export, the official Soviet agency through which a Russian with, say, family icons could sell to the West. But NovoExport had no established policy for dealing art to the West. They sold it to Satra basically as a favor for doing as much business as Satra did. Besides art, Satra also dabbled in the Russian cultural world and, for example, bought the world rights to Sergei Bondarchuk's film *War and Peace.*

We made the following deal with the Satra Corporation. We would advise them on acquiring the art, which we would then catalog as "Property of the Satra Corporation, officially acquired from NovoExport, Moscow, U.S.S.R.," and conduct the sale. We'd then split with Satra whatever profit was made.

So there was a slight seam through which art was seeping out of the Soviet Union. An old church in Moscow renamed Bolshaya Polyanka (big warehouse) was NovoExport's repository of icons for sale. In one antechamber, icons were lined up like books. The irony of icons being sold in a former house of worship was certainly not lost on me the first time I visited. Nor was the fact that there was a tremendous markup between what the Soviet agency paid the individuals who came in with their family heirlooms and what we Americans paid for them.

By the time I went to Russia with my two colleagues, I had been assiduously studying the language, which made my work a lot easier and gave me a more profound access to the culture and its idiosyncrasies. Moreover, I spoke Russian well enough to deal directly with the agents at NovoExport with whom I was working. They would put whatever they wanted to sell on a table in front of me and name the price, and I said yes or no. If we paid $800* for a piece of enamel, in their books they'd mark $100 under the consignor's name. The government would get $600, and there would be $100 unaccounted for, which obviously went to NovoExport—I used to call it Lenin's 10 percent.

Even though I knew that the individual consignor was getting the shaft, there was little I could do or say if I wanted to keep supplying my Russian sales. One time, however, I was unable to keep my mouth shut. We had paid $23,000 for a bunch of gold and silver coins that had been in storage in the Hermitage. At auction in America they brought $60,000. The Soviets were hardly foolish; they managed to keep tabs on what we sold things for. And the guy who had sold these coins to me in the Soviet Union suddenly disappeared. On my next trip to Russia, I asked for him at NovoExport and I was told, "He's no longer with us."

I said quite boldly, "Does it have anything to do with the fact that we made too much money on the coins?" They actually nodded. And I said, "What I made on the coins doesn't

*In 1969, the dollar and the ruble were traded at a ratio of 1:1 in official transactions. On the black market, however, sometimes the ratio went as high as 15:1 in favor of the dollar.

even come close to what you and the commission shop are making off the Soviet citizen. That's more outrageous."

"Never mind," said the official. "That's not the way we look at things."

If I was able to sell for $1,000 a certain piece of porcelain or an icon from one trip, by the next trip a very similar piece would be priced at $2,000. Finally, the prices were so high that we ended up making no money, so we stopped doing business with the Soviet Union through Satra.

But perhaps the greatest source of inventory for my first sales of Russian works of art was a very special private collector. One day shortly after I went to work at Sotheby's, I was holding a tray full of Russian enamel in the elevator. The doors opened at one of the lower floors, and in walked a very striking dark-haired woman. She glanced shrewdly at the enamel and then fixed me with a guileless stare. "That looks like some nice Russian enamel," she said. "Why do you have it?"

"Because we're doing a sale in Russian art," I said.

"I didn't know you did sales of Russian art."

"It's all rather new," I said a bit sniffily.

"Oh, because I have a lot of Russian art myself that I could easily sell."

Though I was already picking up something charismatically infectious about her, I remained for a moment in my supercilious mode. "And who are *you*?"

"I'm the wife of the Lebanese ambassador to the U.N."

She was wearing a positively tattered cloth coat, and I puckishly said, "Well, you're certainly not dressed like an ambassador's wife." I nearly added, "You sound pretty American to me," but managed to hold my tongue.

She answered me with a candor I wasn't quite prepared for. "Well, I *have* to dress like this during the daytime. In order to protect myself. Why, just the other day the Brazilian ambassador's wife got mugged. She was wearing a fur coat, and they ripped it off her back and stole her handbag. I don't want that to happen to me. I like to go wherever I please."

She was telling the truth. This woman, as it turned out, was indeed Ambassador Ghorra's wife. I had observed her at Sotheby's functions, but I was used to seeing her in furs. Now, as she stood before me, she looked as if she hadn't two nickels to rub together.

Olga Ghorra was renowned in New York diplomatic circles for throwing lavish parties, at which she dressed very glamorously. In fact, the Lebanese Embassy was a wonderfully neutral meeting place, in many cases the only place where emissaries and diplomats from otherwise embattled countries, such as Red China and the United States, could be in the same room at the same time.

At any rate, I was invited to the embassy residence, which was then at Sixty-sixth Street and Madison. It was filled with icons and Russian furniture, silver and porcelain, that she had collected during the early sixties, while her husband had been the Lebanese ambassador to the U.S.S.R. under Khrushchev. Mrs. Ghorra and I spent a lot of time together over the next few years; I handled a lot of business for her, and we became very close friends. She was old enough to be my mother, and she and the ambassador had never had any children.

Olga herself had an intriguing background. She was a Lebanese American whose family owned car dealerships in California. As a young woman during World War II, she worked for the United States Army, where she was recognized as being their fastest typist. She was clocked at approximately 150 words a minute on a manual typewriter. Then she met Edward Ghorra, who was then a top Lebanese diplomat to the United States.

And once she married him, he got posted to Moscow, where for a diplomat's wife, life certainly had its drawbacks, and she became bored.

And so she began to collect.

She had a great empathic manner and an irresistible laugh, and the Soviets loved her, even the commonest folk. In this way she got to know the people who ran the commission shops, plying them with cartons of Marlboros and bottles of good whiskey, ensuring that they would put the best pieces of art aside for her. Thus she circumvented official channels, often meeting her contacts in the back of Russian Orthodox churches, where similarly wrapped packages were exchanged. On the black market, she was able to transform $100,000 into 1–1.5 million rubles.

She was generous, she was shrewd, and she did provocative things that people dreamed about but would never dare undertake. For example, since the eighteenth century, one has needed an internal passport to travel anywhere in Russia. And diplomats and their wives were certainly expected to stay put in Moscow. This didn't sit well with Olga Ghorra, who approached Madame Vertseva, the minister of culture, and said, "We're all bored, we don't have anything to do. Can't we go on some trips?" She was flatly refused. Shortly thereafter there was a cocktail party that Khrushchev attended. Olga waited until Madame Vertseva was standing next to the Soviet leader, and then she approached. "You know," she said to Khrushchev, looking him squarely in the eye, "some of the wives and myself would like to look at other cities around here, but we're not allowed to." She then glared at Madame Vertseva.

"Well, I'll fix that," Khrushchev told her.

Mrs. Ghorra subsequently flourished in Moscow and other parts of Russia and kept collecting until 1964. When Brezh-

nev deposed Khrushchev, the Lebanese government trans-
ferred Edward Ghorra to Czechoslovakia as a gesture to the
new Soviet government. This presented a problem for Mrs.
Ghorra, who, unbeknownst to her husband, had filled up the
top three floors of the Lebanese Embassy in Moscow with her
voluminous acquisitions. She told me that she casually announced to her husband, "Oh, by the way, Edward, I have a
few things upstairs."

Ghorra was so blinkered by his diplomatic work that he
never bothered to make a reconnaissance mission upstairs. He
relegated to Olga the responsibility of having the furniture
moved.

Edward Ghorra was the least of Olga's worries. After all,
she still had to smuggle all her treasures out of the Soviet
Union. Armed with a good smuggler's instinct, she began
bribing every official who would have anything to do with
her transport. She decided to move her bounty by rail and
ended up filling three boxcars and riding "shotgun" with them
from Moscow through Leningrad and into Finland, where she
put most of it in storage before continuing on to Czechoslovakia. Theoretically, her belongings weren't supposed to be inspected at any of the borders because she was a diplomat. But
three boxcars was a vast quantity, the sort that would attract
attention, and she had had the foresight to provide herself with
a safe-conduct. A year later, another foreign diplomat was not
so perspicacious, and many of his staff were arrested when he
tried to leave with a score of Russian national treasures.

Before I arrived at Sotheby's, if someone such as Olga
Ghorra came in with Russian things, whoever was there when
she arrived would catalog her possessions, assigning them to
one sale or another, without much thought. But now she called
me, as did other collectors, and pretty soon some of the peo-

ple in other departments of Sotheby's alerted me to Russian objects they knew about. I likewise bowed to their areas of expertise. The age of specialization was beginning. Sotheby's was metamorphosing from a moribund operation that sold only estates to one that was offering specific sales in specific categories for specific collectors.

But the idea of specializing, of catering in a more mainstream way to the client, was galvanized by two events that occurred on the contemporary art scene. The first was the sale of Andy Warhol's *Campbell's Soup Can with Peeling Label* for $60,000 in May 1970. And the second, no doubt inspired by the financial triumph of the first, was the October 1973 auction at Sotheby's of some fifty selected works from the collection of Robert and Ethel Scull. This was the first time that such a large sampling of contemporary art, work less than ten years old, had been put up for auction.

The Sculls, wealthy owners of several fleets of yellow taxicabs, had amassed quite a collection of contemporary art. One of their more significant acquisitions was a work by Jasper Johns: a pair of Ballantine ale cans cast in bronze and set loosely on a bronze plinth. The Sculls, who had bought the ale cans from the Leo Castelli Gallery in the fifties for $950, sold them in the 1971 auction for $90,000. They also sold a snow shovel autographed by Marcel Duchamp for $12,000.

The sale caused an uproar. Three-quarters of the way through, Robert Rauschenberg publicly attacked the Sculls for making so much money on the blood of artists.* Outside Sotheby's on Madison Avenue, a group of disgruntled downtown artists picketed the event, hawking snow shovels identi-

---

*As a result of the Scull sale, Rauschenberg engaged in a quixotic mission to carve out a percentage on any resale of art to be remanded to the artist.

cal to the one that bore Duchamp's autograph. "You can buy these at a hardware store for nine ninety-nine," they shouted to bystanders. "Why pay twelve thousand?" The notoriety of the sale, the high prices paid for art, began to change perceptions. After all, art is legitimized by the marketplace, by the fact that several people are willing to pay large prices. At the time, there was a tendency for the general public to believe that the sudden infusion of money into the art market was happening primarily in the categories of contemporary and modern paintings. And yet a flurry of interest in one area often inspires interest in other areas. The collectors of modern and contemporary paintings were just more visible than equally ardent, if less visible, collectors of Oriental art, porcelain, and eighteenth- and nineteenth-century French, English, and American furniture. Many people felt that the Scull Sale of Contemporary Art was the nadir of the art world, but many others, including me, believed that it was just the beginning of a strong market in many different categories of art.

5. Shopping in Moscow

I journeyed to Russia three different times: once in 1969, with Marcus Linell and Peregrine Pollen; once alone, in '70; and once in '72, with Francine LeFrak, now a film producer, whose father is the well-known real estate investment tycoon who built Lefrak City. Every trip to Russia was made for buying decorative arts and icons in tandem with the Satra Corporation, in particular John Kapstein, who loved the idea of strafing dingy warehouses for imperial goodies to be recycled at a Sotheby auction. When we weren't working, John dragged me to the theater and the movies.

An American touring Russia was a rarity in the early 1970s. Even though I had a bona fide reason—I was on a buying expedition—there were nevertheless a great number of restrictions on where one could and could not go. And having a tour guide was pretty much de rigueur. On my very first day in Leningrad, in 1969, I was led around by a woman with a two-dimensional personality, who spewed out Communist-slanted Russian history like an automaton. Unable to bear her monologues, I insisted upon trading her in for a more engaging companion and was given a five-foot-three troglodyte named Alex Smolsky.

Alex met me at my hotel, the very grand pre-Revolutionary Astoria, and quite capably and patiently led me through the enormous Hermitage Museum, the 1,200-room edifice that Catherine the Great built for her painting collection, as well as the adjacent Winter Palace, which together take up nine full city blocks. Alex spoke very good English. He was well educated—his mother was a curator at the Hermitage—and our relationship was rather energetic because, like many literate Russians, Smolsky was dying to know more about the West. I, in turn, was eager to learn more about his country.

Before I left for my 1970 trip, I wrote Alex a letter saying that I was again coming to Leningrad for a week; he managed to meet me again, and we did some more traveling around together when I wasn't combing warehouses for good icons or traipsing through secondhand furniture stores. Never was I under any illusions about Smolsky. He was a tour guide, and I knew that the tour guides were required to write up their clients and turn in the reports to the KGB. By the end of my second stay in Leningrad, I had grown weary of his company. There was something a bit unctuous and eager about his personality, which began to grate on me after long days of enforced companionship.

And so, when I was contemplating my third trip, I figured I could at least start out by trying to get along on my own. I had already established contacts in the icon warehouses and the consignment shops; by then my study of the Russian language had advanced a bit, and I was able to do some reading and make simple conversation. And besides, I would have Francine LeFrak for company.

Francine and I flew over together in July 1972. We were what I'd call good acquaintances at the time, but after spending two weeks together we became best friends. (Traveling in the Soviet Union will make any two people either best friends or enemies.) From the airport in Moscow we took a cab to the Nationale, a hotel on Red Square that I'd fallen in love with the first time I visited. From the window of my room there, I had watched, albeit from a distance, a man ceremoniously opening the French doors to Saint Basil's Cathedral.

The moment we arrived at the Nationale, we learned that for some odd and inexplicable reason, Francine had been booked into a different hotel, the Rossiya, on the other side of Red Square. The Rossiya is a ghastly example of modern institutional architecture. It has five thousand rooms and until recently was the largest hotel in the world (the Soviets loved to brag about this). We immediately tried to rectify the matter but were told there was no room for Francine at my hotel. Not that they necessarily would've known if all the rooms were indeed booked.

I had already discovered that their large hotels, like certain other Russian institutions, operate in a very chaotic manner. I thought the disorder was perhaps intentional, a way to keep foreigners off balance. You had to pay very close attention to the little unimportant things. If you were staying in Room 1496, it wasn't necessarily on the fourteenth floor. In fact, Room 1496 might be located on the eighth floor, next to 8756. In this way, I suppose, the Soviets created a constant bureaucratic diversion that made it more difficult to see the bigger picture.

Francine began to panic, and I knew that my only recourse was to dip into my bartering supply. Since much of the tourism of the Soviet Union was run by women, my supply was weighted that way. I had arrived in Moscow with an entire suitcase filled with good nylons, perfume, and Bic pens (Bic pens were craved by bureaucrats, who had trouble acquiring ballpoints, which they desperately needed in order to fill out the standard quintuplicate forms). The customs official inspecting my luggage had given me an odd look and taken notes.

I now reached into my bartering suitcase, pulled out a bottle of Pierre Balmain perfume, and went in search of the stalwart woman who was the hotel manager. I told her how wonderful everything was and gave her a bottle of perfume, compliments of John Kapstein, who was a faithful patron of the Nationale. I then had to praise the hotel where Francine had been given a room and explain that it would be a lot more convenient if she was located close by, instead of on the other side of the square.

Without missing a beat, the manager said no, the Nationale was absolutely booked up. I pulled out another bottle of the perfume and told her this gift was from me and how happy I was to be staying in this marvelous hotel. She blinked at me coquettishly, then picked up the phone, barked at someone in Russian, and finally said in English, "We happen to have one room available, without telephone." As she didn't have lots of friends to call locally, Francine moved hotels.

I have always appreciated good colognes and perfumes, but now I understood a bit more about their value. If you wanted tickets to the Bolshoi Ballet, little bottles of Fabergé cologne worked very well. They could get you to the front of the ticket line. Soviet people spent so much of their lives standing in line; it seemed almost like an instinct. Whatever there was for sale, even it if wasn't needed, could probably be bartered later on for something one did need.

Going out for dinner in the Soviet Union was a utilitarian affair. The meals were served at large tables, Viennese style, and you found a place and sat next to people you didn't know. Most Russians would bring along plastic bags and scavenge any extra food for future meals at home. There was very little choice; you had to eat what they put before you. I had neglected to explain this sufficiently to Francine. The moment we sat down, she foolishly tried to adhere to her strict low-fat regime and ordered a green salad, no oil, with vinegar and mustard on the side. I laughed at her. A salad? In my three trips to Russia, I had seen lettuce only once. Lettuce was pretty much a black market item. What the Soviets had in abundance was caviar. We ate plenty of that during our two weeks.

We managed to spend a few days in Moscow and then took the midnight train to what was then Leningrad.* We alighted from the train at eight in the morning, made our way to the hotel, and who should be standing in the lobby but Alex Smolsky. He claimed to be passing through the hotel. This, I knew, was a total fabrication. Any Russian native seen mingling in a hotel that catered to foreigners was risking arrest. The moment was rather awkward, and Smolsky had a nervous grin plastered on his face.

Scrambling a bit, I explained to him that I felt I knew the town well enough and that I'd been studying Russian, so that Francine and I really had no use for a tour guide. He looked completely crestfallen and said that nevertheless he would like to spend some time with us. And so to get rid of him for the

*My Russian teacher recently said, "I was born in Saint Petersburg, I went to school in Petrograd, I grew up in Leningrad, and I went back to Saint Petersburg."

moment, I invited him to come to dinner with Francine and myself a few days hence, on Thursday. He asked if he could bring a friend, and I agreed quickly in order to end the conversation.

Thursday rolled around, and Alex Smolsky showed up at the appointed place with a godlike, six-foot-two blond named Slava Petrov. Although Slava spoke broken English, he managed to amuse us during dinner. Beyond being a knockout, he was actually quite a cultured man. He claimed to be a dentist and to have a dacha on the Gulf of Finland. Francine and I were so enthralled with Slava that we invited the two men to accompany us to the ballet the following evening.

July in the far north of Saint Petersburg brings on "white nights." The sunlight doesn't even begin to wane until 10:00 P.M., and there's dusky twilight until 2:00 A.M., when the sun rises again. I remember stepping out of the Maryinsky Theater at well after ten in the evening and looking at the way the slant of light struck the apertures of the building, the way the whole city was bathed in a golden wash. It felt like four o'clock in the afternoon. The thing about the midnight sun is that the great profusion of light makes you feel supremely energized. And after having just seen the incomparable Kirov Ballet, a company for which Slava Petrov claimed to have danced, I was up for adventure.

At this precise moment, Smolsky turned to me and explained that a friend of his had once maintained a correspondence with the playwright Edward Albee but had recently lost touch with him. He asked, on his friend's behalf, if I would be so kind as to take the playwright a letter. I hesitated. Albee was a very distant acquaintance—he probably would not even remember having met me. But also, given the nature of Soviet paranoia, I had a lot of trepidation about carrying a missive out of the country, engendering a correspondence that might be judged by the Soviet authorities as subversive. I didn't say no, however, and when Smolsky suggested that the four of us go to his friend's apartment, I agreed. There was no denying, my adventurous spirit aside, that I enjoyed being able to look at Slava Petrov. And both Francine and I were willing, even motivated, to prolong the viewing.

We got into the car I had hired and drove to a large apartment building, grand by Russian standards. Francine and I exchanged a look of caution; we assumed there had to be some kind of KGB connection. The man who was waiting to greet us was a tall, distinguished-looking fellow in his mid-thirties named Gennady Schmakov. His apartment had many rooms and was full of books.

Schmakov bade us come in and served tea. Our arrival seemed to put him in a highly nervous state. Schmakov explained to us that he wrote movie reviews, a sort of Kafkaesque job, because he was obliged to expound the Communist party's "aesthetic" opinions. The reviews, he explained wistfully, were freighted with Soviet condemnation. In fact, he had just previewed *Slaughterhouse Five* but had no one to talk to about it. Clearly, his private view was quite different from the one expressed in his written critique. And once Francine and I realized this, it occurred to us that he was an unlikely sort to be a KGB affiliate. Nevertheless, we were careful around him, though he seemed thrilled to have us in his apartment.

Schmakov, Francine, and I spent several hours of spirited conversation, until two in the morning. Leningrad is a city of islands connected by a series of bridges and canals, and at 2:00

A.M., when most people are asleep and the traffic is almost nil, all the bridges go up to allow the easy passage of goods and other necessities over the waters. It occurred to me that we would now be stuck for several hours in Schmakov's apartment, and I suddenly felt trapped.

Schmakov stood up and motioned for Francine and me to follow him into another room. Once the door was closed, he told us *sotto voce* that he was convinced Slava Petrov was bona fide KGB. Schmakov wanted to talk to us about various other matters but could not do so in front of the other two. He suggested that the three of us go for a walk, but I thought that would seem too suspicious. So I encouraged him to go off with Francine.

Their private conversation, I learned later, was almost entirely concerned with how Francine might use her Jewish mafia connections to help get the Panovs, the Jewish ballet dancers who were members of the Kirov, out of the country. Meanwhile, I went back into the living room with Alex Smolsky and Petrov. In the midst of the most banal conversation about traveling, Alex stood up and walked over to Slava. He proceeded to sit down on Slava's lap and confessed to me that he and Slava were lovers. Because I had never given them any indication that I might be gay, I shot them a dubious look. "Is this some kind of KGB setup?" I asked.

Both of them looked at me, agape. "KGB?" they repeated simultaneously.

"I'm not stupid," I said. "This has got to be a setup. You're making an assumption here. We've never discussed this sort of thing."

"Maybe not, but I just want to tell you what's what," Alex Smolsky said.

"All well and good," I said, "but what on earth does it have to do with me? Unless, of course, you're going to tell me that you're willing to leave me alone with your friend," I said to Smolsky, glancing at Petrov.

Smolsky shook his head resolutely and reiterated that he and Slava Petrov were lovers, something that I found difficult to fathom.

"Well, I don't know what the point of this evening is," I snapped. "Except if you're trying to find out for the 'file' if I'm gay. And if you are, believe me, it's no secret. My family know I'm gay. My business associates know I'm gay. On the other hand, if you're trying to cook up an arrest for an 'illegal activity,' I haven't done anything. And if you have me arrested I'll get to improve my Russian, which is something I wanted to do anyway."

This seemed to disarm them, and their behavior changed appropriately once Francine and Schmakov returned from their subversive walk. There was no sexual punch line that evening, the last one I ever spent in the Soviet Union.

Because of the strangeness of that encounter, and the threat of a possible future KGB entrapment, Francine and I decided that we should probably cut short our stay in Leningrad and undertake the next leg of our journey—to Paris. We returned to our hotel from Schmakov's, me bearing the letter for Edward Albee, packed up our suitcases, and kissed the Soviet Union good-bye.

The moment we arrived at the Hôtel de Crillon, Francine lay back on her bed, picked up the telephone, and asked room service to bring her some caviar.

I looked at her, aghast. "All we've been eating for the past two weeks has been black bread and caviar."

"I realize that, Robert. But now I want caviar back in my life as a luxury, not as a staple."

※ ※

Shortly after I returned to America, I received a letter written in careful English from Slava Petrov (obviously he'd had it written by someone). Announcing his intention to study Japanese, he asked me to send him Japanese-language primers, in return for which he'd send pictures of himself playing sports. I assume he thought I was hard up.

I was much more interested in helping Schmakov, who, before we left his apartment, pleaded with us to get him out of the Soviet Union. He seemed like a kind, compassionate man with an intellect that was keen to be nourished by the scholarly resources of the West. To try to help him, Francine and I threw a cocktail party to raise money. It was our idea to send an American woman over to the Soviet Union to marry Schmakov. In fact, he was already married, to a woman who had an excellent job as the head of the musical comedy theater in Leningrad, but because he was so desperate to get out of the country, his wife agreed to give him a divorce so that he could go through the motions to acquire American citizenship.

We found a suitable American woman, and she traveled to the Soviet Union, where a marriage ceremony was performed. The newlyweds returned to New York to live in her apartment. Then, unfortunately, she fell in love with Schmakov and didn't want to go through with the preordained divorce. And this had to be resolved; shortly after Schmakov arrived, he announced to me that he was a homosexual.

Once Schmakov sorted out this second divorce, his life vastly improved. After hearing somebody muttering the word "schmuck" in the street, he changed his name to Smakov, thinking it would sound more attractive. He managed to make some very influential friends. Bearing in mind that many highly educated people escape the Soviet Union only to find no work in their respective fields in America, and often settle for the most menial jobs, Smakov's Western life, by comparison, reads like a fairy tale.

He was practically adopted by Alexander Liberman, the head of Condé Nast Publications, and his wife, Tatiana. Meeting them at a Russian expatriate gathering, he so charmed the Libermans that he was invited to come live at their house and be their cook. Smakov cooked for a while, met a few more people, made a few more contacts. The next thing I heard was that he had landed himself the job of writing a biography of Mikhail Baryshnikov, who had also become a good friend of his. After Baryshnikov, he chronicled the life of another Kirov defector, Natalia Makarova. At the height of his life in the United States, Smakov was at the center of the Russian expat community. But then he contracted AIDS, much to the sadness of all his devoted new friends, and he died before he could finish his most ambitious project, a complete history of the Russian ballet. By the time he died, he had been living in the United States for ten years.

Francine and I were devastated by the loss of our friend. We had grown fond of him, we'd delighted in watching his life bloom in America. It seemed tragic that he had come so far against such great odds only to die before he could complete his life's work. Which is not to say that one death is more tragic than another. There was just a certain irony about Smakov's fate. We never managed to contact his wife and child in the Soviet Union; they may still believe he's alive and living in America.

More than a few people have suggested to me that Francine and I should never have intervened as we had in Smakov's life. It pained both of us to hear that reaction. For more than anything, I have come to believe that you cannot measure the quality of a life by how long it lasts. And I say that despite the way Smakov died, those ten years he spent in America were infinite.

6. Fragility 101

When I give the orientation talk to all new employees at Sotheby's, one of my questions is: What are three things beginning with the letter *d* that are good for the auction business? The answer is death, divorce, and debt. To a lesser degree, one might add a fourth and a fifth: disease (terminal, usually) and discretion. And that's why our business is extremely fragile and volatile. In fact, my orientation talk is called Fragility 101.

If somebody has just died and you're called in to do an appraisal, you must be conscious that every bereft family has its own sensibilities about that moment in time. The various emotions require careful consideration, as do the legal and logistical aspects of the valuable art, decorations, and furniture of the deceased. There may be charitable heirs, there may be family fights, and we have to be able to sort out all the details and peculiarities in order to proceed. The challenge for an auction house such as Sotheby's is to be able to conduct business somewhat aggressively—there is competition for every estate and every sale—but also to use tact and restraint.

In late 1994 I received a "did you know them" sort of phone

call from our trusts and estates people. A valuable collection belonged to a dealer in medieval and Renaissance works of art, whom I'd known for as long as I've been in the art auction business. Leopold Blumka had died some time before, and his wife, Ruth, who took over his business, died in the autumn of 1994. Mrs. Blumka was a wonderful woman, one of the great characters in the art world. And her final idiosyncrasy was that she left no instructions about who should get her things, propelling her family into a conundrum over the dispersal of a sizable collection of art. I attended the funeral as well as the burial and paid my respects to her son, Tony, and his wife, Lois, who worked at Sotheby's until recently. Because of that connection, I assumed that we would at least be called in for advice.

But then we received a phone call from Tony Blumka, informing us that Christie's had been to see them about the estate, and where were *we*, as though Christie's had beaten us to the punch. I went to visit Tony Blumka in the company of Dede Brooks, the New York–based president of Sotheby's World Wide, as well as George Wachter, the head of the department of old master pictures; Elizabeth Wilson and Margie Schwartz, the heads of the European works of art department of New York and London respectively; and Warren Wietman, the executive vice president involved with trusts and estates. The moment we walked in the door, I told Tony very directly, "You know where we are. You know that if you needed help, you could call. I just thought it would be inelegant to approach you before you were ready to make practical decisions about the estate. I figured that whenever you were ready you'd pick up the phone." That put him at ease.

It was one of those situations where I assumed we had the bases covered, as it were, but Christie's had come after the

Blumkas a bit more aggressively, which made Sotheby's seem too laid-back. We're not in the least bit laid-back. We try not to chase ambulances if we can help it. And yet despite the fact that Sotheby's had the psychological edge, Christie's still went after the estate.

I don't intend to give the impression that we are necessarily holier than Christie's; there are, however, many times that we lay off for reasons of ethics and elegance. Personally, I think Christie's is sometimes too keen to get business. But don't get me wrong: I'd happily undercut Christie's. They do it to Sotheby's often enough.

In the case of a divorce, because a household is being dissolved, Sotheby's provides a serious service to people who are no longer in love. But we often get embroiled in the fast liquidation of assets. Obviously, you cannot cut the Monet down the middle and say, "That's your half and this is my half," but you can divide the money. We once had a Fabergé imperial egg that came up for sale as the result of a divorce. It had been purchased in Switzerland some years earlier, for $198,000. The divorcing couple put it up for sale, and it was purchased by Malcolm Forbes for $1,760,000, the thirteenth Fabergé egg he owned.

I've been in tense situations where an estranged couple are practically trying to kill each other across a crowded room in the middle of an auction. In the early seventies, a well-known couple was struggling through an extraordinarily acrimonious divorce. Linens, Louis Vuitton trunks—there wasn't anything they didn't argue about. The only people who survived the debacle unscathed were the lawyers on both sides: they made a bundle. The collection was predominantly contemporary art; there wasn't much else of theirs to be sold at auction. Fervent collectors of contemporary art often don't collect much else.

However, their matrimonial agreement stipulated that each spouse be allowed to bid during auctions; in effect, this meant there would be a 50 percent discount to re-own the picture, since the proceeds were being divided between them. As a result, there was a great deal of tension at all the sales. And if, for example, Mr. knew Mrs. was going to bid on something, he might bid against her out of spite, to increase her cost and make more money for himself.

Debt is self-explanatory. If you need money, you sell what you can to pull yourself out of dire straits. The best example of a sale we did for reasons of debt involved a man named Jack Dick. In 1974, Mr. Dick lived in Greenwich, Connecticut, in a huge pile that is now the residence of Harry and Leona Helmsley. Jack Dick was what I'd call a financier who sailed close to the wind. He owned Blackwatch Farms, in Goshen, Connecticut, with a herd of four hundred Black Angus cattle.

At that time, people in the highest tax brackets were constantly looking for and finding all sorts of shelter schemes. Mr. Dick had one of his own, in which people could put down a deposit of, for example, $30,000 against the purchase price of $600,000 on a stud bull and begin taking depreciation deductions off the total $600,000. Jack Dick would fly prospective investors up to his farms, meet them at the Tarmac in a limousine, convey them to his farm, and show them examples of the herd. Justifying the high price of the Black Angus bull, he'd demonstrate how the bull semen could be withdrawn to impregnate the cows. Jack Dick also sold Black Angus from farms all over the country. At his office at Goshen, there was a map of the United States, into which he stuck pins to show where the other animals were. A lot of very savvy people invested with Jack Dick. He made millions of dollars by taking

Blackwatch public and selling his shares in the company. Then the company went bankrupt.

In the early seventies, Mr. Dick was told by the IRS that he owed them $7–$8 million in back taxes. In addition to this manacle of debt, there were lawsuits pending right and left from the parties who had invested in the Black Angus. This litigation contributed to the eventual tightening of the tax laws, including regulations regarding the deductibility of farm estates.

Just after I was made head of the European furniture department at Sotheby's in 1972, we received a phone call from Mr. Dick. His house was full of wonderful English furniture and sporting paintings. Because I was newly appointed in my job, the higher-ups at Sotheby's in London wanted to make sure I had the proper support to give an aura of confidence. They asked the head of English furniture in London, Michael Webb, to come over to America to help me.

Michael and I spent one entire morning looking around Jack Dick's mansion and coming up with estimates. Though he had many pieces of furniture, the best part of the collection was the nineteenth-century English sporting pictures, including works by Gainsborough, both Herrings (*père* and *fils*), Stubbs, Wooton, et al. These were pictures of, for example, Lord whoever's favorite horse, usually with a little dog at the lower left and a groom holding the horse's bridle. Jack Dick had paid a lot for many of these paintings; indeed, the market for them had been created by his competition with Paul Mellon, another avid collector of this genre.

Mr. Dick liked to feel that he could work the dealers down, and he had developed the reputation of being what is called a "slow pay." Everybody in the trade had grown used to this.

The moment he waltzed into an antique store, the dealer would jack up the retail price. Dick, as he was wont to do, would bargain fiercely for a discount, and they'd grant it. So he wound up paying retail. Then it took months for the dealers to get their money out of him. On the other hand, he was a wonderfully generous host, who, in his heyday, invited hundreds of people to the estate, gave them horses to ride, organized enormous bacchanalian sleigh rides during the winter, and generally did a lot of heavy entertaining.

Once Michael and I finished combing through the enormous house and had conferred privately, Jack Dick led us into an ornately furnished dining room, where a lunch of eggs Benedict was brought to us by liveried servants. I found the grand style rather ironic, given the fact that this man was seven or eight million dollars in debt to the government. Nevertheless, probably because I was so young and earnest, between bites of my eggs I demonstrated that I had enough temerity to tell the unvarnished truth. Knowing that he claimed to have put $2.5 million into furnishing the house, I said, "If we sell the contents of the house, not including the paintings, we're looking at a return of between seven and eight hundred thousand." Jack Dick, a lean, distinguished-looking man with salt-and-pepper hair, stiffened in his chair, and his eyes popped as though he were being strangled. "Why?" he gasped.

Coolly continuing to eat my eggs Benedict, I explained. "For example, I know you spent $250,000 on carpeting the place, but the carpeting is broadloom and it's not worth a bean to have it pulled up." I went on to say that the beautiful early-eighteenth-century Canton enamel table that he had bought for $38,000 was worth probably $10,000 to $15,000 at auction; that the Chippendale mirrors in the entrance foyer were worth a third of what he paid for them. Luckily, I had Michael

Webb backing me up, and Michael was older and a bit more tactful.

And yet I was right on target. The sale of pictures was done in three sessions over two years; the recession and the oil crisis of the mid-seventies hit right in the middle of it. The first sale, in April 1975, brought in over $1 million and was a success. The house portion brought $700,000 (the Canton table sold for $16,000).

We put together a three-volume hardbound set of catalogs for the paintings, which were sent to London to be sold and in and of themselves ended up bringing well over a million dollars. The great irony of Jack Dick's life was that the day we sent him a check shortly after the first sale, he suffered a heart attack and died. I had the unfortunate task of repeating my lunch conversation to his widow, who was still running on the impression that, excluding the paintings, there was $3 million worth of stuff in the house.

In terms of the lesser *d*'s, disease, particularly now in the age of AIDS, has encouraged several people I know to have auctions while they are alive. It is somewhat like attending one's own funeral, in the strictly material sense.

The last category, discretion, refers to owners' selling something because they think the market is right. During the late eighties, when the Impressionist market was being underwritten by the Japanese, the famous collector and former secretary of the Treasury Douglas Dillon began to consider selling his Monet. He conferred with David Nash, the head of Sotheby's Impressionist and modern painting department. When Mr. Dillon asked David, "What would you think my Monet is worth?" David looked him straight in the eye and said, "Probably eight million."

This was a picture that Mr. Dillon bought in the 1960s for

perhaps $200,000–$300,000. And he decided, at his *discretion,* that the difference between what it cost him and its value in the current market was profound enough to allow the picture to disappear off his wall. And we did sell it for $8 million— luckily, before the Japanese stopped spending their billions on Western art.

In dealing with any art sale or estate sale, an auction house such as Sotheby's will try to take a cut from both sides of the activity. From the seller, or consignor, a certain percentage, ranging from 6 percent to 20 percent, is usually taken from the gross receipts of the sale. This is used to cover the cost of putting on the sale, including verification of authenticity by experts, catalog description, as well as printing the catalog (which can be extremely costly) and advertising. Then there is the regular buyer's premium, which is set in stone and never changes: the buyer is charged 15 percent of the purchase price up to $50,000, 10 percent thereafter. But we don't always take the full seller's commission. Sometimes, if the idea of doing a certain sale is prestigious enough so that we feel the exposure would be good for business, we have had to scale down the seller's commission.

One of my favorite stories about commission involves competition over the estate of Marietta Tree in 1992.

Marietta Tree was born into the Boston Brahmin Peabody family and was twice married: first to Desmond FitzGerald, of the CIA; and second to Ronnie Tree, the financier. Marietta Tree's brother, Sam Peabody, is married to Judy Peabody, the AIDS activist, who happens to be among my three closest friends in the world.

Sotheby's decided not to pursue the estate of Marietta Tree, because the then chairman of Christie's, Daniel Davison, was her first cousin. This was a great act of restraint, because before this cousin had been installed as Christie's chairman, Sotheby's had traditionally sold art and furniture for the family. We would've loved nothing more than to handle the estate. I could quite easily have called up Sam Peabody and insinuated myself into the competition. But we decided, What's the point? Let Christie's have it.

Christie's went through their motions. They inventoried Marietta Tree's various works of art and furniture and came up with their estimates. Then one Saturday morning out of the blue, I received a phone call from Sam Peabody, who was at Marietta Tree's apartment with her two daughters, Frances FitzGerald, the well-known author, and Penelope Tree, who in her day was a famous model. Sam told me that the man who was buying the apartment had made offers to buy some of the furniture; this would be in lieu of sending the furniture to be auctioned. The family had already received Christie's itemized appraisal but were seeking "additional advice" to know whether or not the man's offers were appropriate. I told Sam that I'd be very happy to give advice regarding the offers, but the quid pro quo was that I would like Sotheby's to make a proposal for the selling of the Marietta Tree estate. Sam spoke to the daughters, who agreed.

I arrived at the Sutton Place apartment a few days later with some of our English furniture experts. In the end, the experts and I agreed that Christie's had estimated everything properly and the buyer had made a respectable offer. Then I turned to Frances FitzGerald and said, "Now I will make a proposal to sell your mother's things. I liked your mother very much. She often put me at her table whenever the Citizens Committee for New York had their benefit. Obviously, we didn't pursue this estate because of your family connection to Christie's. But I would love to do it. It would be very prestigious for Sotheby's.

And for that I'd offer to charge the estate a zero percent commission." I hesitated. "But then again, I'm sure that since Christie's is practically family, they've offered you a similar deal."

Frances FitzGerald's mouth dropped open. She said, "Well, no, frankly. They're charging us 6 percent commission plus insurance, shipping, and illustration costs."

I quickly pointed out that totaling those costs translates approximately to a 10 percent commission from the seller's side. And then I added, "That isn't exactly what I'd call a family rate. Nevertheless, I still won't charge you anything."

"Well," Ms. FitzGerald said, "you may have this sale after all."

"I honestly don't think so," I told her. "In fact, I think I'm going to save you a lot of money. Trust me: the moment you tell Stephen Lash, the executive vice president over there at Christie's, that Robert Woolley offered to charge you zero commission, it'll take him a split second to match it. If I'm wrong about this, I owe you a case of champagne. But if I'm right, you owe me a case."

The next day, a case of champagne arrived at my home. The Marietta Tree estate brought in nearly $700,000, which meant that I saved the two daughters around $50,000. And the upshot of the story is that now whenever Frances FitzGerald has anything to sell, she calls me. And whenever she gives me something good to sell, I always send her a case of champagne.

7. Local Treasures

One of the ways I learned to hone my instincts was a program that Sotheby's invented more than twenty years ago, called Heirloom Discovery Days. HDDs, as we used to call them, were created specifically for the younger experts, such as myself, who were rising through the company and needed on-the-job experience in dealing with the public. For me, Heirloom Discovery Days were like logging in vital hours for pilot training.

On HDDs, we went out in search of hidden treasures that were owned by folks who didn't necessarily know what they had. We usually made these junkets in cooperation with a local art museum. Six or seven experts in various fields—silver, porcelain, Oriental art, paintings, furniture—would travel together. The institution that sponsored our trip usually threw a Friday night cocktail party for its patrons, who would bring in, say, their grandmother's Dresden vase for appraisal. If we got lucky on Heirloom Discovery Days, the local TV station would come by and take footage of us inspecting the wares of people waiting anxiously for the good or bad word.

We'd install ourselves behind tables in a town hall or in the more spacious wing of a museum—if there was such a place. People clutching their precious heirlooms would pay a five-dollar fee, which was given to the sponsoring institution. They would form lines in front of the category that corresponded to their possession. The appropriate expert would give an oral estimate. I manned the miscellaneous line, which was more diagnostic, set up for people who weren't quite sure what they had. I found the miscellaneous line appealing. I like surprises.

You'd spend the day talking to as many as a few thousand people. And if someone was bringing in something Aunt Tilly said was very expensive, which since her death had sat on the mantel, you didn't want to burst any bubbles. If an item was valueless, I tried to explain that this style or object was not presently fashionable but that trends were changing all the time and a few more years might see an increase in price.

One Heirloom Discovery Day, a woman handed me a little plate that was painted with a bunch of cherubs in clouds. I inspected the plate carefully—it didn't have any defining mark—and flipped it over, then asked her how many more she might have. This question seemed to inflame her, and from past experience I geared myself up for what might be coming next.

"Any more?" she said huffily. "Why, this is the only one."

"Well," I said, "since you have only one of them and it's not marked, it's probably French, mid-nineteenth century, and worth somewhere in the neighborhood of fifty dollars."

She was a rather diminutive woman, as I remember, with a helmet of iron-gray hair coiffed short and wavy. She leaned toward me, her eyes black and beady like a hawk's. "You're an idiot!" she said.

"Excuse me?"

"You're a complete idiot. You obviously don't know what you're talking about."

"And why do you say that?" I asked her, as evenly as I could. After all, no one enjoys having his intelligence so publicly and vociferously impugned.

She said, "I know how many generations it has been in the family. And because of that, I know it's been in the family long enough to prove that my ancestor brought it over on the *Mayflower*."

The woman was suffering from a common misconception. Many people count back generations in terms of forty to fifty years each, which is not really accurate. In the decorative arts world, we have found that a generation is closer to twenty years. So if this woman had figured that the porcelain went back six generations, she was calculating back three hundred instead of one hundred fifty years.

I smiled politely. "Would it change your mind if I told you that the *Mayflower* sailed one hundred years before porcelain was invented in the Western world?"

"No, it wouldn't. I know it came over on the *Mayflower*, and that's all there is to it."

"Well," I said, "let me give you your five dollars back. You obviously know more about this plate than I do."*

On the miscellaneous line I received the people who

---

*Porcelain as we know it didn't make its appearance in Western culture until kaolin was found in Dresden in the early eighteenth century. Prior to the discovery of this clay in a river, porcelain had been made only by the Chinese, who cloaked the formula used in its manufacture for 400 years. At one time, armies could be traded for bits of porcelain; it was more expensive than gold. Today, however, in certain Greek restaurants, they crash plates to the ground.

thought they had a Stradivarius, an Amati, or a Guarneri violin. I used to address a crowd of people and say, "How many of you have Stradivariuses?" Up would go a bunch of hands. "How many of you have Guarneris?" Up went others. It was always amusing, because I knew the odds against discovering genuine late-seventeenth- or early-eighteenth-century instruments. There are only around eight hundred Strads in existence. However, the Germans made thousands of copies in the nineteenth century, with facsimile labels and even eighteenth-century dates. When people hovered around me with their instruments, I would say, "You probably had a great-grandfather who bought this thing a hundred fifty years ago, and you've treasured it ever since. And frankly, you can continue to treasure it, because it's undoubtedly a very well made instrument. Make sure it's played." In the hundreds of Heirloom Discovery Days I've participated in, never have I stumbled upon a Stradivarius.

I did discover a very important icon in 1979, when I was tending to the miscellaneous line in Rochester, New York. One of my colleagues came over to me holding an extraordinary late-fourteenth- or early-fifteenth-century icon of Saint George that measured two by three feet. It was right up my alley, if you will. Exhilarated, I identified the painter as from the school of Andrei Rubloff. Icon painting was theoretically monastic and anonymous, and Rubloff's is one of the few names that are known.

The couple had purchased the icon in the estate sale of a doctor who had worked on famine relief in the Soviet Union during the 1920s. Though they were unable to identify the icon precisely, they had had the good sense to recognize its quality and paid $2,500 for it, a lot of money for a couple who were living off a university professor's salary. Unfortunately for

Sotheby's, my identification only served to convince them to hold on to it. They donated the icon ten or fifteen years later to the University of Rochester and took a tax deduction of around $500,000.*

And that was a reason why the Heirloom Discovery Days weren't really profitable for us. When people found they had something worth auctioning at Sotheby's, they often ended up holding on to it even more fiercely. Though HDDs did help the local museums raise money, they didn't generate an enormous amount of business for us. Certainly not enough to justify the fact that at one point during the seventies we had sent three teams to over 150 cities. It was like a military campaign. I even had a map in my office, where, like Jack Dick, I'd keep track, with green-headed pins, of the HDD invasions of the American hinterlands.

There were a few memorable HDDs, to be sure. I remember one we did on a beautiful day in May at the top of the steps at the Philadelphia Art Museum. I stood there and watched literally thousands of Philadelphians slowly wend their way up those famous stairs, some clutching paper bags, others holding pieces of silver that caught the sunlight and glinted like razor blades. We discovered one of Edward Hicks's paintings of *The Peaceable Kingdom,* which we sold for $488,000. At that moment, blowing away family legends and traditions was raised to the level of art.

Jim Lally, who had been the head of Chinese art at Sotheby's, happened to attend one of our HDDs in Lake Oswego, New York, when an unassuming older man loped into our diag-

*Luckily, they took their deduction before 1986, when the tax laws changed that would have limited deductions to the amount of the original purchase price.

nostic center with a paper bag. The moment he took a blue-and-white shallow porcelain bowl out of the bag, Jim Lally did an inward double take. "Where did you get this, sir?" he asked.

"Off the dining room table. We've been using it as a fruit bowl since the mid-thirties. We found it in the attic of my parents' house, which I inherited and now live in."

Lally proceeded to inspect the underside of the bowl, where he found an old auction label. And after a bit of research, we were able to verify that this was, as Lally suspected, a piece of Ming porcelain that Parke-Bernet had auctioned in a sale of William Rockefeller's estate in the 1920s. It had sold for $6.50; in 1980, we auctioned it for $76,000.

Perhaps because there is so much everyday porcelain around, we often forget that there is still porcelain of exceptional quality and provenance. Such was the case with a group of nuns who called Sotheby's from the convent of Saint Elizabeth Seton in Yonkers.

The convent possessed some Old Master pictures, which the nuns wanted to sell in order to fix their roof. A group of us went up to see what they had: paintings of turgidly religious subject matter, which had, unfortunately, been rendered valueless by the nuns' feeble attempts at restoration. The nuns served us tea, and in the midst of giving them the unhappy news, Joseph Kunst, the head of the European arts department, picked up the sugar bowl and nearly fainted.*

Kunst (his name is the German word for "art") noticed on the bottom of the bowl the underglazed blue mark of the Duomo in Florence and the capital letter *F*. What the nuns had on their hands was a unique piece of porcelain that be-

*Joseph Kunst died of AIDS ten years ago.

longed to one brief period under the Medicis in the sixteenth century, when they founded a factory and made a so-called prototypical porcelain copy of a Chinese tea bowl. Kunst said, "Well, forget about your Old Master pictures. Here's your roof."

Only once before in the twentieth century had a piece of Medici porcelain been sold at auction—and wouldn't you know, it was the very same bowl. The bowl had been donated years before to the convent by the man who had purchased it in 1910 for $200, a good price then, considering it could have bought you a third of a car.

I remember that when the bidding for the porcelain bowl reached $40,000, one of the nuns in the front row popped her rosary beads. I finally brought the hammer down at $180,000. I also remember that when we were a day late with the payment, we received a call from the convent, inquiring about interest. No good deed ever goes unpunished.

8. The Recluse

In 1974, I became a senior vice president and head of decorative arts. Part of Sotheby's decision to promote me had to do with the fact that by presenting myself as a maverick of change, I anticipated trends in the buying and selling of art. But I had also been blessed with the serendipity of being in the right place at the right time. For whenever my predecessor, Edward Lee Cave, moved up in the company, I always followed behind. Edward is now one of the top real estate brokers in New York.

There wasn't a tremendous amount of competition for the decorative arts post, and yet I feel that I was tailor made for it. I believe that in the art business as well as at Sotheby's, gay men actually have an advantage over straight men, who usually have wives and children and are not as free to pick up and go off to investigate a possible consignment halfway around the world. I was mobile, my schedule was quite flexible, and I was willing to go anywhere at a moment's notice.

In my everyday life I have always been quite forward about being gay, and admittedly it has turned some people off, but in my business I also knew how to put on wrist braces.* I could blend with straight men. Flying out to Scottsdale, Arizona, to look at a collection of French furniture, I could read the sports page and talk to the men I was meeting for breakfast about the local football scores.

Shortly after I was promoted, John Marion came to me and said that he'd had a golf game with a banker from Fidelity Union Trust of New Jersey, who told him about a woman whom they'd been taking care of financially for the last eleven years. Apparently, Mrs. Dodge had suffered a stroke and was being kept alive on machines, with round-the-clock nurses. The banker had shown John an inventory list as thick as a phone book: some great American paintings and other superb collectibles. All of the appraisals, however, were outdated and vastly undervalued, and if you didn't look very closely, the collection seemed of little worth.

When John Marion first mentioned Mrs. Dodge, there was something familiar about the name, but nothing registered until he and I took a drive out to her estate in Madison, New Jersey. And then it came back to me full force. Of course I knew who she was. The 140-acre Drew University campus, where I'd gone to college, was contiguous to Mrs. Dodge's 450 acres. Mrs. Geraldine Rockefeller Dodge. I used to know her "from the other side of the fence."

Geraldine Rockefeller Dodge lived in a gabled, gloomy mansion on an estate called Giralda Farms, between Morristown and Madison. Her house was situated on one corner of the estate; and her husband had lived in a Federal-style house on the diagonally opposite corner. Although they lived sepa-

---

*Wrist braces are imaginary devices that gay men put on in the morning to stop their hands from going limp.

rately, she'd be taken every Friday in a horse-drawn surrey to have tea with him. And every Friday at Drew there was the inevitable question: "Should we go over and watch Mrs. Dodge do her drive-by?"

I had seen her from afar: a somber woman, a great recluse who dressed completely in black—black veil, black gloves, black coat. She owned only black cars. When she married Hartley Dodge in 1909, they were considered one of the richest couples in America. It was a combination of dynasties: she was the daughter of William Rockefeller—John D.'s brother— and Hartley Dodge's family owned the Remington Arms Company in New Haven. They had one child, Hartley Dodge, Jr., who moved to Paris as a young man. In 1931, he received a car as a gift from his father, and shortly thereafter he drove into the Seine and drowned. Although John Marion discovered a letter to Mrs. Dodge that showed Hartley junior to be a very morose young man—it could have been a suicide missive—perhaps it's better to say that he died under mysterious circumstances.

Mrs. Dodge never got over it. She stopped living, or more precisely, she began living in a time warp. In the emotional devastation that followed her son's death, Mrs. Dodge went into mourning for her life. No one knew, in light of the fact that Hartley senior had given Hartley junior the car, whether this precipitated an estrangement between the parents. In any case, Geraldine Dodge stopped living with her husband, who moved to the other house on the estate. The last time anyone from the public had been invited to the estate was for a dog show in 1936. After that Mrs. Dodge went into complete seclusion and devoted the rest of her life to her dogs and to collecting.

When Mrs. Dodge had her stroke in 1964, 186 dogs were

living in her kennels. A ramp went from the ground floor to her bedroom, and every night eight different dogs would sleep with her. The rotation system she employed was scaled down over time; it had to be, obviously, because she was not of sound enough mind to orchestrate the changing of the dog. By 1975, when she died, only two dogs were left. In her will, $20 million was bequeathed to the Cornell University School of Veterinary Medicine to research and study hip dysplasia in German shepherds (her favorite breed). She bequeathed 10 acres of her land and $10 million to create Saint Hubert's Giralda (Saint Hubert is the patron saint of hunters), now one of the preeminent animal shelters in the United States.

At the bank, there was some serious jewelry, including D-flawless diamonds, clusters of diamonds with black pearls, and all the other main-event colors: blue, red, and green. There was a bag of gold coins. I presume that before Mrs. Dodge took up seclusion, she received lots of glittering gifts from her husband.

When John Marion and I arrived at Giralda, we were overwhelmed by the inventory. There were something close to four thousand bronzes, almost entirely *animalier*. Whole rooms had been devoted to her bronzes; they were lined up like soldiers. I was immediately concerned that such a profusion of bronzes coming up for auction might flood the market. Let's face it, not many people are clamoring for *animalier* bronzes. But there were lots of American paintings, and all kinds of sculpture— also of animals. Mrs. Dodge's obsession for collecting animal art was unlimited and quite simple. If it had an animal on it, she bought it.

On that first visit, Mrs. Dodge was still being kept alive in a state of suspended animation. I remember seeing her in bed, her eyes open and focused vacantly. Almost as though she knew that her effects were being reappraised, she died shortly after we finished our evaluation. And then the bank told us to prepare the house for the auction.

John Marion said to me, "Woolley, it's yours. You're in charge of this whole operation. You're the *capo primo.*"

To auction an estate requires a tremendous amount of preparation. We make a proposal to the executors and draw up a contract with the estimated costs. We figure out what experts need to be called in. Here, one expert was called upon to work tirelessly—the person who knew *animalier* bronzes, Barbara Deisroth, head of the twentieth-century design department. A lot of the operation had to be geared to her other work. We then arranged the objects in three categories: two thousand lots were to stay with the main body of the auction, which we decided to hold right there at Mrs. Dodge's mansion; another thousand lots of paintings and some of the more important bronzes were to be sold later, in Manhattan; and the rest was relegated to what I had conceived to be a grand "tag sale."

For each object we had to provide a description, and this meant literally holding the object, looking at it, recording its condition. Then we created a title, identified, if possible, the artist, pinpointed a date, wrote descriptive copy, which varied from a few lines to a few pages, depending upon the importance of the item. Measurements were taken and decisions were made whether or not to illustrate each piece in the catalog.

And then we determined the range of the estimate. In most cases we compared the object to similar pieces that had been sold recently. Before I came to Sotheby's, the estimates tended to be higher and more elusive. It was as though the prestige of the auction house was being factored into the price and driving it upward. Once I arrived at Sotheby Parke Bernet, I began trying to rescale the estimate, to redefine the idea behind the estimate, to target an estimate that was more within reach of at least a group of collectors in the room who would say, "For that money it's mine."

In the fifties, there was one estimate list at Parke-Bernet, which was guarded assiduously by a woman named Miss Duckworth. If Miss Duckworth liked you she'd be helpful; if she didn't, tough luck. In the late sixties and early seventies, estimates were never listed with the objects in the auction catalog; they weren't even in the catalog but rather were loose pages that were made available to prospective clients. Our staff was instructed to be a little bit coy before answering the question of what a piece was worth. They had to determine first if they thought you could afford it. Admittedly, it was not a very good marketing skill, and I insisted that we make it easier for people to buy what's on offer.

Fortunately, by the time the Dodge sale came about, the estimates were being printed and bound in the back of each catalog. It wasn't until ten years ago, after I'd rattled the cages until everyone was sick of it, that estimates were put immediately under the description of each object. The only thing that still drives me crazy is that sometimes when we offer something unique or worth millions, we use the phrase "estimate on request."

In one of the talks I now give to new employees at Sotheby's, I describe each step in the process—from when an object is first consigned to us until it is finally sold—and how much care is required in the handling. To illustrate, I pretend we have been given my pen to be auctioned, and I ask everyone to count how many times I pick it up and put it down by the end of my lecture. If they have followed me closely, the number is around twenty. And this is for the most ordinary thing that gets illustrated and put in the catalog—not an impressive work of art that might travel to Chicago, Los Angeles, Paris, or London to be exhibited before it is auctioned.

We have a union of Teamsters who are responsible for moving items between departments, private residences, and the salesroom. The Teamsters also do the physical chores that are required to create an auction exhibition. They are a group of highly dedicated employees who are, in many ways, the bedrock of the company. In New York City alone, 250,000 things get picked up at least twenty times, which translates to millions upon millions of well-executed logistical activities. The majority of mishaps actually occur in the hands of prospective buyers. However, once an object comes into our hands, it is insured against loss at the "median estimate."

The Dodge estate was more high-maintenance than usual, and most objects were moved many more than twenty times. Items were shifted from one room into another because of limited space. There was interminable photographing. Many things were packed up and put on trucks and sent into Manhattan.

The great educator of the Dodge Estate was the bronzes. And even our expert, Barbara Deisroth, came away knowing a lot more about this nineteenth-century art form than before. Dodge's bronze collection was as good as it gets. It was encyclopedic. Many of the bronzes she bought were made by Antoine Louis Barye, the most popular French sculptor in the last century. Sculptors such as Degas, Rodin, and Barye made their models in clay or terra-cotta, and then the bronzes were cast by a foundry. Barye hovered around the foundry to make sure they came out right, so the bronzes produced during his lifetime were considered more valuable. But in a literal sense, these bronzes were not his autograph but rather his conceit, his idea. I would much rather own a maquette; only there can you see the artist's fingerprint. Barye's studio was purchased on his death by the Barbedienne Foundry, which continued to cast his work but marked it accordingly. These products, of course, are less valuable.

Since bronzes generally come in multiple editions and are fairly easy to copy, it is important to separate the genuine article from the imitations. We compare the size of the signatures. If one piece is already authenticated and another comes along that is slightly larger than the original, you know it's been recast. The same holds true with a slightly larger signature— then you know a casting has been made and the second piece is either a fake or an unauthorized replica. If, however, you examine a bronze and find the name is misspelled, it probably *is* an original; after all if you were going to fake something, you'd be careful not to misspell the artist's name. Misspelling could, conceivably, be the fault of a foundry worker who might have transcribed the signature incorrectly when the bronze was first cast. If you don't care about authenticity, it's easy to find copies of bronzes advertised in the back of such magazines as *Gentleman's Quarterly* and *Esquire* for a fraction of genuine prices.

Most of Mrs. Dodge's bronzes had been purchased through the Graham Gallery on Madison Avenue. The Grahams will say that Mrs. Dodge kept them alive during the Depression; she was virtually the only major client they had. She was very exacting, but they depended on her business. One of her caveats was that whenever she visited during the summer, the air-conditioning had to be turned off hours before she arrived, no matter how hot the day.

Once we began our work, I was met each time I went out to Mrs. Dodge's estate by a man who worked for Fidelity

Union Bank. Herbert Ball had been the bank's guardian of Mrs. Dodge for eleven years. Though she was in a coma, he spoke to her every day; he felt she heard him. Herb was extremely protective of Mrs. Dodge's property. I found out rather quickly that though Herb Ball was a nice enough guy, his anal-retentive gene was activated whenever I wanted to investigate objects in display cases. He kept an enormous brass key ring that was perhaps a foot in diameter. It held the keys to all the rooms, as well as to all of Mrs. Dodge's display cases, which he often seemed reluctant to open, even though I told him I had only a few weeks left to figure everything out. I preferred to unlock everything and leave it open.

It turned out that Mr. Ball loved Lhasa apsos, Tibetan "lion dogs." Apparently, he had a few of his own. One day I happened to bring along my handsome Lhasa apso, Hank. Mr. Ball was so enraptured by my dog that he completely forgot to monitor my activities. I discovered that all I had to do was bring Hank along with me, and Herb would gladly hand over his brass ring of keys. Herb and Hank would go off—literally for hours. They had 450 acres to explore.

While they were gone, I spent a lot of time drifting in and out of rooms. Practically every room in Mrs. Dodge's enormous house had a crucifix in the appropriate corner. And there were hundreds of rosaries—every time I opened a drawer, there was another rosary. When we were about to let people into the estate, we called a press conference. I told the reporters how I had unearthed all the crucifixes and rosaries, which indicated that Mrs. Dodge had, at some point in her life, converted to Catholicism. The moment I said this, William Rockefeller, who was standing there with me, interrupted and said that she was buried as an Episcopalian. I almost responded, "I don't care how they buried her; she wasn't *with* us for eleven years." There's no doubt in my mind that this woman was a converted Catholic.

One of my great fascinations was the soap room in the attic, a fifteen-by-fifteen-foot room full of wire-cloth shelves that pulled in and out and were full of soap, thousands of bars of soap in all the different brands. An old high-WASP contention held that airing soap would dry it out and make it last longer. The soap was never put in the sale. The bank gave the Sotheby's staff permission to take it home, which is what we all did. I may even have one bar left of Pear's glycerin soap. Mrs. Dodge never got rid of anything. She couldn't even throw away the silk ribbon from gifts. It was ironed and rolled on tubes with a cross-stitch at the end.

I may have been able to get Mr. Ball out of the way, but I did run into some small interference from one of my colleagues, Joan Washburn, who was head of American paintings at Sotheby's. The object of our disagreement was a nearly ten-foot bronze statue, by the American sculptor Cyrus Dallin, of an American Indian holding a bow. Mrs. Dodge had commissioned this unique cast, called *The Passing of the Buffalo,* in 1931 and had paid $12,000. The heroic-size sculpture was set in the middle of her land, on a massive boulder. It was my thought to remove this bronze, take it into New York, and put it in the lobby of Sotheby Parke Bernet on Madison Avenue. There it would become the figurehead or mascot of the Dodge sales in Manhattan. Although it was expensive to move a piece this enormous, I felt the bronze would attract publicity and generate the appropriate buzz. But Joan Washburn said, "No, no, it makes no sense. Leave it in the house sale, Robert—it's too big and it's not really worth all that much money." She had given an estimate that was slightly more than what Mrs. Dodge had paid forty years before.

But I had this hunch, and I've been known to dig my heels in, even with the experts who are supposed to know more than I do. I just told Joan Washburn that I was going to have the sculpture moved and that was that.

Mrs. Dodge also owned a town house at East Sixty-first Street and Fifth Avenue, next to the famous Knickerbocker Club. The house looked as though it was surrounded by a small forest. During the Depression, Mrs. Dodge had bought the two adjacent town houses on one side of her and one house on the other side. These she had torn down so that when she brought her dogs in from New Jersey, they had a place to roam.*

Her town house had been decorated in a Florentine Romanesque style and was furnished with excellent nineteenth-century French furniture. But strangely, the low ceilings and the overall melancholy of the place reminded me of a Methodist seminary I might have come across when I was a child. Lugubrious. In fact, when you walked in at the servants' entrance, the first thing that greeted you was a bronze copy of the lid of her son's coffin—a kind of anonymous death mask. It wasn't the best way to greet someone, but then perhaps her point was to discourage people from hanging around.

When I explored the town house, I found some excellent furniture and some exquisite nineteenth-century paintings, but the most exciting find was in a closet off the dining room. There I unearthed a few crates that were stuffed with ivory-colored newspapers from the thirties; I sensed that I'd stum-

---

*After Mrs. Dodge's death, when the land was sold and her house was leveled to make way for a high-rise building, her great-nephew Nelson Rockefeller had the architect step back the new structure an extra twenty feet so that his view down Fifth Avenue from number 810 would not be interrupted. He had the clout of a being a Rockefeller, coupled with the fact that at the time his great-aunt's house was being demolished, he was governor of New York.

bled upon a real treasure. When the crates were carefully removed to the galleries and then opened, we found a rather
stunning carving in Carrara marble of an utterly lifelike Benjamin Franklin. On the back, it said: "J. A. Houdon, *fecit* 1784."
This was among two or three busts that Jean-Antoine
Houdon, the celebrated eighteenth-century French sculptor,
had made of Ben Franklin. This image of Franklin has become
so well known throughout the world that it is almost a cliché.
The Metropolitan Museum has one of Houdon's bronzes,
which they believe is an autograph. But all our experts agreed
that Mrs. Dodge's was an original autograph work, as opposed
to a copy, of which there were many.

I also found a bust of Houdon's daughter Sabine. I later
learned that Mrs. Dodge had paid $2,800 for the Ben Franklin
and close to $30,000 for the Sabine. Part of the reason why
Mrs. Dodge had paid so much more for the bust of Houdon's
daughter had to do with a feeding frenzy started by the British
dealer Lord Duveen, an important international figure in the
art world, who, among many accomplishments, sold Henry
Clay Frick the majority of his collection. A few years after
Mrs. Dodge made her exorbitant purchase, Lord Duveen auctioned yet another Houdon bust of Sabine, which brought several hundred thousand dollars, a tremendous amount of money
for the early 1930s, equivalent to something like twenty million dollars in today's currency. I feel that Duveen manipulated
the market. Even though Mrs. Dodge spent a lot more for the
Sabine than for the head of Franklin, we adjudged the Sabine
to be a copy, not an original. Mrs. Dodge had left both busts
in their crates and probably never saw either one again after
she bought them.

Mrs. Dodge kept all her auction catalogs and dog-eared any
page where she bought something. While the men were mov-

ing things, I'd go through her catalogs and take note of the dog-ears, to see if the objects she marked were still actually in the collection. She was quite idiosyncratic. For example, there would be a dog-ear at an oil painting by Meissonier, a nineteenth-century French painter—usually of soldiers or boulevardiers—marked at $1,200. The next page might be a nice little Renoir, priced at $450, but no dog-ear. In hindsight, one would be tempted to draw attention to what seems like very poor judgment. But Impressionist paintings didn't start raking in major money until the late 1950s; in the mid-1930s, no one cared about Impressionism. Mrs. Dodge was a connoisseur of the art that was popular in her day.

She loved Rodin; she owned perhaps twenty of his bronzes—including the famous ones: *The Kiss, The Thinker*—and even a sculpture in marble, which is quite rare.

The house sale exhibition began on October 4, 1975. Almost ten thousand people a day came through, many of them out of curiosity. After all, Mrs. Dodge had been a famous recluse for forty years, and her mysterious house had been off-limits to the rest of the world. We couldn't flood the house with people, so we pitched a tent in the backyard and created a holding area, allowing five hundred people at a time into the house. We had to hire two hundred guards to help control the flow of visitors. We managed to keep them happy by offering coffee and indicating as best we could how many more hours they had to wait. Word of mouth spread, and people kept showing up to see the place. At the house sale, people were allowed to touch whatever objects were on display; the experience was tactile and intimate as compared to, say, the Frick Collection. You had a sense that these objects were in transit; on their way to finding new owners, they had been orchestrated into a brief, temporary arrangement.

The first lot of the house sale was a set of nine silver-plated serving dishes and a bowl. It was a onetime Sotheby's tradition for John Marion to buy the first lot, which he did for $125. Afterward he gave me one of the pieces, a Tiffany silver-plated tray, which he had inscribed: "From Lot #1 to Bob Woolley, who made it all happen."

◖◦ ◦◗

The Cyrus Dallin American Indian was estimated at $15,000–$20,000 and auctioned in New York on Halloween of 1975. John Marion auctioneered rapid bidding up to $60,000, where all but two bidders dropped out. One was the late Arthur Rubloff, who was in the midst of building yet another of his shopping centers in Chicago—called, as chance would have it, Indian Creek. Rubloff thought it would be tony to buy the ten-foot sculpture and put it at the front of the shopping center, crowning the parking lot.

The competition was a man from Muncie, Indiana, Edmund Petty, whose great-aunt, in 1929, had commissioned a Cyrus Dallin bronze of an American Indian, to be erected in the town in memory of her husband. Now Petty wanted to buy Mrs. Dodge's Indian bronze to commemorate his father. For an auctioneer, it was a perfect setup: two people who suddenly wanted to own the same thing, and they both had *a lot* of money.

Mr. Petty was sitting demurely up in the balcony, Mr. Rubloff was in the front row. Rubloff had been buying bronzes throughout the sale. Petty had bought absolutely nothing. When the bidding edged up to $100,000, the room hushed. Both men remained poker-faced and kept bidding without any hesitation whatsoever. Then Arthur Rubloff hesitated and

Mr. Petty earnestly bid $150,000. "I have one hundred fifty thousand," John Marion said. "One hundred fifty thousand dollars." When the gavel came down, we had added a zero to Joan Washburn's estimate. Magnanimously, she congratulated me.

Shortly after the sale, I received a telephone call from Mr. Petty. Quite matter-of-factly, he said, "Mr. Woolley, I would like the boulder."

"Come again?"

"I need the boulder the statue was standing on."

I laughed. "You must be joking."

"No, no, I want the boulder. If it means negotiating with the bank, I'll do that."

"Can't you find a boulder closer to home?" I couldn't help asking.

"It wouldn't be the same," he said.

I rang up the bank and told them what Mr. Petty wanted, and they said, "If the man wants to pick it up and take it to Muncie, that's his privilege. Just as long as we don't have to pay anything and nothing on the estate is disturbed."

So Mr. Petty hired a crane to move the boulder, which weighed many tons. He had to have a special railroad car built to haul it back to Muncie. He had all the markings of a true collector: he had focused on acquiring one object, but perhaps in the end he had been too focused. We never heard from him again. As far as I know, he never bought anything more, proving again one of my clichés: "If you get a crazy price for an object, the first time is an accident, the second time is a trend, and the third time is a market."

The same type of spectacular competition began again when the Houdon marble bust of Benjamin Franklin came up for sale. On one side you had a consortium of American painting dealers who were trying to buy the piece for the White House; on the other you had the British Rail Pension Fund, which had set aside £12 million a year to be invested in works of art. Sotheby's had been acting unofficially as consultants for the fund, and we had recommended the Houdon.

The irony of this piece was not lost on the British bidders: Benjamin Franklin, who was the American ambassador to the court of Louis XVI, ending up bleeding the French economy to pay for our revolution, which caused King George III to lose the colonies and Louis XVI to lose his head. They secured the bust for $310,000—thirty times more than the original estimate. The bust has since been lent to the Getty Museum, where it is now valued at $5 million.

As a final note to the Dodge sale, I arranged a tag sale on the property, to dispose of some of the lesser-valued items and curios. It took four days and four pickup-truck loads to ferry everything from the house and attic to the stables, which I had cleaned out for the sale and filled with folding tables to hold trays of goods. There were double damask linen napkins by the dozens, which we priced at $5 apiece; interminable boxes of Christmas decorations; furniture from the maids' rooms. The most expensive item was an ancient sable stole, which sold for $250. There were hundreds of pairs of shoes that Mrs. Dodge never wore; women with size five and a half feet were doubtless in heaven. At one point I spotted Joan Lunden, now of *Good Morning America,* waiting in line, and I quietly and undemocratically ushered her out of the line and into the tag sale. To her I must've been like Saint Peter at the Pearly Gates: she wore a size five and a half.

There were also a great many examples of Gustave Stickley furniture, American Arts and Crafts pieces produced in the nineteenth century. I've always derisively called it "porch furniture." In fact, that's what it was at Giralda. In 1975, hardly anyone thought it had much value. I saw Andy Warhol waiting patiently in line with his checkbook and said, "Hello, how are you, nice to see you, follow me." I slipped him in at the side. Andy began buying the Stickley pieces for $75, $100, $150 apiece. When he got through with his little shopping spree, there were none left.

9. My Great Love

In 1974, the year I was made head of decorative arts at Sotheby's, I had the great good fortune of meeting the love of my life, Jeffrey Childs. I have always been grateful that Jeffrey's previous lover was bearded and balding and looked vaguely like me. The man was an antique dealer in New Orleans, and Jeffrey was involved with him for eight months until he came home one evening and found the man *in flagrante delicto* with a previous lover. Jeffrey's emotional style was such that he was on an airplane at seven o'clock that night and never went back. That's the way he was.

Jeffrey and I lived in the same building, 12 East 97th Street. But since we had never been introduced—he knew who I was, and I certainly knew who he was—we were merely nodding acquaintances who sometimes rode the elevator together. In those years, there was an Upper East Side gay bar called Harry's Back East, which unfortunately no longer exists. I remember seeing Jeffrey there and thinking to myself that he was so good-looking he could go up to anybody in any bar and say, "Okay—you," and the man would be thrilled. He was six feet one, with broad shoulders, light-brown hair, and celestial blue eyes that had an exotic cast, and he had a prepossessing manner. It never occurred to me that he'd even consider anybody like me.

One night we were each at Harry's and engaged in just a little bit more than our usual salutatory exchange. When nothing else was happening for either of us, I said, "Do you want to share a cab back to the apartment building?" At some point after that, I said, "Perhaps you'd like to *see* my apartment." Admittedly this was not the most original line in the world, but that was as far as I could go. Sexually screwed up as I was, I could never be the aggressor in a relationship.

That night, one of the straight men whom I'd been pursuing, the sort of guy who did everything gay people do but wouldn't kiss—"Kiss you? You must be crazy. I'm not queer"—happened to phone while Jeffrey was sitting in my apartment. Brian wanted to come over. A bird in the hand . . . Well, when I got off the phone I told Jeffrey he'd have to go, but he stubbornly refused to leave and kept talking to me until the doorbell rang. Months later, he told me that he had stayed to see the competition. Anyway, these two men, Jeffrey and Brian, passed each other in the night.

Jeffrey's interest in me was fueled by that first casual rejection. It was the sort of rebuff that rarely happened to him, and once he left my apartment and went back to his own, his ardor was piqued. The next afternoon, a Friday, we met again and we made love, and after we made love I went alone out to Fire Island, where I was staying with Thierry Millerand, whom I had just hired to be the head of French furniture at Sotheby's. The moment I arrived in the Pines, I told Thierry, "I've just met the person I'm going to live with for the rest of my life. He hasn't a clue, of course, but I've been looking at him for three years, and finally we got together.

"He's encumbered by family money," I went on. "And I'm going to marry him." And I did.

We were both incredibly acquisitive—it was one of the ties that bound us. We loved things. The first night I met Jeffrey, he told me that he had a little jadeite bear made by Fabergé. Now, I had been trained in Russian works of art, and judging whether or not something was Fabergé was one of the things I could do. "I'd like to see it," I said, knowing that I was running the risk of being the messenger who gets killed. But then he said to me, "Granny bought it for me for my twenty-first birthday at A La Vieille Russie."

I was stunned, but I managed to say, "Well, if you bought it there and they told you it was genuine Fabergé, it probably is. When was this that your grandmother bought you the jadeite bear?"

"In 1967, right before I went to Vietnam."

"Do you remember who the salesman was?"

"No, why?"

"Because at that time I was working at A La Vieille Russie."

The next day, I called the Schaffers and asked them to look up the invoice. It had been written in my hand; *I* had sold them the jadeite bear. Saying the bear was Fabergé was being a bit imaginative with the truth. The invoice stated that the bear had been made in the Imperial Lapidary Works in Ekaterinburg during the Fabergé period. It was not Fabergé, but as soon as Jeffrey took it home, it *became* Fabergé.

I certainly remembered the grandmother, Mrs. Constance Crimmins Childs, but ironically, I didn't remember Jeffrey. I recalled that there had been a choice between the jadeite bear and a malachite falcon. Apparently, Mrs. Childs had given Jeffrey a budget of $1,000 for his birthday. They had been fighting over the past few months, and this gift and a lunch at the

Plaza represented their rapprochement. Jeffrey had been extremely close to his grandmother. They spoke every day until her death, in 1973. Mrs. Childs had been small of stature but exuded a kind of hauteur that said, Don't mess with me!

The jadeite bear was $450 and the malachite falcon was $750. Jeffrey, like Mrs. Dodge, whose estate I was handling when I met him, loved anything small and animal-like. It didn't matter if it cost two million dollars or two bucks. He should've bought the falcon, which was much more interesting and had been carved by Edward Sandoz, a very famous French sculptor of the Art Deco period, whose work, incidentally, has since greatly appreciated. Unfortunately, Jeffrey wanted an object *and* some cash, and the bear would afford him more cash. So in one way, he made the wrong choice.

Jeffrey's mother is Sandra Hitchcock Childs, whose grandfather was one of the founders of Reliance Electric Corporation of Cleveland. In 1930, she married Frederick R. Childs, whose family on his mother's side (the Crimminses) owned the land at 625 Madison Avenue on which the Revlon building now sits. John D. Crimmins, Jeffrey's great-grandfather, was an architect-contractor who dug the New York City subway in the late nineteenth century. In those days, whenever there was a building going up, he dug the hole.

The Crimminses, a good Catholic family, were racked with controversy when their son married Sandra Hitchcock, a Presbyterian, and because of this the marriage took place in a rose garden instead of in a church. Although Jeffrey and his brothers were raised Catholic, Sandra has remained a Presbyterian. They all grew up in a compound on Long Neck Point Road in Noroton, Connecticut, which was a stone's throw from the Convent of the Sacred Heart, at the very end. Jeffrey's great-grandfather Crimmins was the one who built the bridge from the mainland to this point. The thirty-eight-room Childs house had been converted during the 1930s from what was once a stables; Sandra Childs built her own house next door in the seventics. So when I say I married up, I mean it.

Jeffrey's family had always known that he was gay; over the years, he would bring home the occasional friend. Until I came along, when any of Jeffrey's gay friends would ring up on the phone, his mother would say, "Oh, a character of yours called." The first time Jeffrey brought me home, we'd been up in Vermont for the weekend and were driving back to New York on the thruway, when on a whim he said, "Pull over, Robert, at exit ten." We then drove the few miles to Long Neck Point Road and dropped in on his parents, who were having dinner, and I was casually introduced.

At the time, Jeffrey was about to spend $5,000 on a Georgian secretary bookcase that I had looked at and realized had been artfully cobbled together: an old bureau bottom and a bookcase top that didn't belong to it, as well as a new cornice. His parents brought up the purchase at dinner, and right in front of them I told him not to buy it. I could see it registering with them: "This one's all right." From then on, Freddie always referred to me as Jeffrey's boyfriend, and he seemed to respect my place in Jeffrey's life. And because my meeting with Jeffrey's parents coincided with my preparations for the sale of the Dodge Estate, whenever I found another set of rosary beads in one of Mrs. Dodge's drawers, I'd give them to Freddie. Both he and Sandra were accepting, but they weren't reconciled.

They, like my parents, always said that if they could magic-wand us into "straight" they would, but perhaps most parents feel this way. "How great to have a gay child!"—who ever hears anybody say that? Back then I was one of the few men in a gay relationship who was truly open about it and expected to bring along my partner whenever I was invited anywhere. Jeffrey was more reticent, and yet he couldn't help but follow my lead. Once I became involved with him, however, I realized that being gay could be incidental in my life; it didn't have to be my central preoccupation. Being gay certainly helped in my business, but I never had to use my sexuality to get ahead.

Jeffrey had gone to Vietnam as a medical corpsman and was shot during the Tet offensive in 1968. He told people that he went to Vietnam for patriotic reasons. But I knew that on some level he was deeply disturbed about being homosexual and wanted to tempt fate. The story went that during Tet, Jeffrey's unit was required to get a body count every night for the news networks. The evening he was wounded was actually his first exposure to a firefight; he had been in Vietnam only a few months.

According to Jeffrey, whenever body counts were asked for, somebody volunteered to go out into the field and get them. To avoid being shot, however, the volunteer would make a guess. Jeffrey, who could be quite compulsive, didn't know any better, and very methodically he went out into the hot zone, got down on his hands and knees, and started counting bodies, his butt up in the air. The next thing he knew, he woke up in the medical tent—he'd been shot in the upper right thigh. The bullet had burst through his groin area and gone out the left thigh, severing his sciatic nerve. In any previous war, he might have died from the wound, but luckily he got picked up right away by a helicopter. He claimed to be haunted by the memory of looking down on himself on the operating table, but that may have been a morphine-induced delusion.

Jeffrey would undergo several agonizing operations on his leg. Ultimately, he couldn't feel anything below the knee, and because his leg muscles had atrophied, he was required to wear a brace. Then one sweltering July day in 1969, he was out by a friend's pool in Connecticut and happened to rest his dead foot on a sun-baked flagstone. He felt nothing until somebody said, "What is that balloon you're standing on?"

The balloon was the fried ball of his dead foot, which had swelled up without his realizing it. And from then on, the condition of his leg was exacerbated by an open wound, which never permanently healed from any of the subsequent skin grafts.

Part of our life together was dealing with that on-going situation. But it wasn't as though he was crippled; indeed, when he was fully clothed, you could barely tell that anything was wrong. He demonstrated a slight hesitation when he walked, but he could dance.

In 1978, he had gone into the hospital for some further procedures on his leg, when the doctors discovered that osteoporosis had set in. The antibiotic they dripped into him to combat it was so inexorably painful that the doctor said, "By the time you're forty, this thing will have to come off."

"Then get it off now," Jeffrey said.

I was in New Orleans on business when he called me from the doctor's office and said quite coolly, "I've decided to have my leg off."

Wearing a prosthetic device was not as easy as Jeffrey had thought it would be. He assumed that he was going to order one, snap it on, and go off like a mountain goat. But at least he had a sense of humor about it. If people Jeffrey hardly knew asked him why he was limping, he'd sometimes pop off his prosthetic leg and mortify them.

One night there was a benefit at the National Academy of Design in the presence of Princess Margaret of Britain. Jeffrey was dancing with another princess, Maria Christina ZuSayn Wittgenstein, and he fell. And when he fell, his prosthesis went literally at right angles to the rest of his body. Princess Margaret rushed over to me, shrieking, "Oh my God, oh my God!" thinking it was a real leg that had split.

"No, no," I said. "Nothing to be concerned about, Ma'am. That's a prosthesis. It snaps right back on."

But by then Princess Margaret had nearly fainted.

I was always bells and banjos in love with Jeffrey Childs, whereas he *grew* to be in love with me. For him, it wasn't the "some enchanted evening" sort of thing. One afternoon in the second year of our relationship, he just said to me, "I think we should stay together, Robert. It all makes a great deal of sense." In 1973, however, it was commonplace to have open relationships, for one lover to say to another, "If you want to go out and cat around all night, that's your business." I myself didn't need to cat around. Fidelity, if you were lucky enough to find it, came to be defined as something beyond monogamy.

We'd go out to dinner on a weekend night and come home, and while I was winding down and quietly getting ready for bed, Jeffrey would be gearing up and changing into jeans. In a state of erotic anticipation, he'd carefully choose a T-shirt to make himself look dazzling for downtown carousing. In the beginning of the relationship, watching him get ready to go out was very painful for me. But after a while I realized that if I was being satisfied sexually and he wasn't, that was *his* problem, not mine. We already knew our lives were seamy; he just had to prove it downtown. And so monogamy ceased to become an issue. Had I made it an issue, I believe that Jeffrey and I never would've lasted.

Jeffrey used to call me the "virgin queen" because I'd never gone to a bathhouse, never had public sex, never checked out the meat rack on Fire Island. Actually, I had gone to the meat rack once, with a friend, but when I showed up in a gauzy djellaba, he looked at me and said, "Where do you think you're going?"

"Well," I said, "aren't we going into a forest?"

He said, "I refuse to be seen with you unless you're wearing shorts and a T-shirt."

For some reason, the idea of sex out in the open reminded me of being in church: everything seemed orchestrated and posed—and it was as much about love as churchgoing was about God.

I have come to believe that gay sexuality is mostly trying on something new all the time. When you're in a relationship, unless you put a great deal of effort into keeping sex spicy, if it's done in a straightforward fashion—pun intended—it can become boring. In my opinion, there is something intrinsically less complementary about sex between men; instead of having two different electrical charges blending, as happens between men and women, the sexual charge between two male lovers, being similar, tends to burn out much faster. This is not an indictment of gay relationships or an argument against homosexual monogamy; it's just a recognition of male body chemistry. As I have observed, men tend to get bored sexually more quickly than women. And if sex is boring, it wanes. I watched myself go from being wildly attracted to Jeffrey, to pleading headaches and having sex with him once a month, to having sex with him every two months.

Once, Jeffrey went down to New Orleans for a few weeks and came back in a foul mood. I kept asking him what was the matter, and he kept denying anything was wrong; nevertheless, for two days he was impossible. Ultimately, I said, "Whom have you fallen in love with?"

"Don't be silly."

"No, no, I know what's going on. You're acting like a horse's ass so you can have an excuse to do something if I get angry. That's not going to happen. So I think you should tell me if you're besotted with somebody."

He collapsed on the sofa and admitted that he'd fallen for a guy in Louisiana who was married, with children.

"Is he going to move north? Are you going to set up house together?"

"No, of course not."

"Are you moving to New Orleans?"

"Don't be ridiculous."

"So what's the problem here? As far as I'm concerned, have a relationship with this man. I know you're not wild about spending money on plane tickets, which means that you might see him once every month or, more likely, once every two months. That's fine with me."

I was so easygoing about it that Jeffrey literally got on the phone that afternoon, called up the man, and confessed that their relationship was hardly going to survive over the long distance. I had unwittingly taken the wind out of their sails.

One rule remained: Jeffrey was allowed to be in lust with somebody else, but not in love.

He was tremendously obsessive about his acquisitions. He used to have a collection of little lead animals on the windowsill above Fifth Avenue. One cold, wet evening, a little dog toppled over, and its tail broke off and flew out the window. This happened only a few minutes before Jeffrey was supposed to meet my boss, Marcus Linell, for the first time. We were going to the theater.

When the tail disappeared, Jeffrey became crazed. The fragment wasn't more than a millimeter long, but that didn't seem to matter. He was certain that it had fallen down into the grating outside the building. Marcus arrived, and Jeffrey barely allowed himself to be introduced. He couldn't consider going to the theater until he got the super and a ladder and examined the inner lining of the grating. The last thing I wanted Marcus Linell to think was that my companion was a maniac.

But Jeffrey was adamant, and he came back twenty minutes later with the missing piece. Luckily, we still had time to make the curtain.

For such whimsies, as well as his maverick way of playing bridge, he was always referred to as being "a piece of work," a real handful. He was relentlessly outspoken. He spouted his opinions and hardly cared how other people reacted to them. His was a built-in self-confidence that came from being moneyed, which in turn kept him from feeling the need to prove himself in the professional world. He never worked the whole time we were together, except for one nightmarish period during the late seventies and early eighties, which I call the "store period."

For five years he ran an antique shop on upper Madison Avenue that specialized in chintz-covered Georgian furniture and Chinese export porcelain. Unfortunately, Jeffrey was much too chronically acquisitive to be a good dealer. Nothing very nice stayed in the store for long; anything truly interesting would be brought home. Sometimes he'd go for an entire month without selling anything; and he'd get so depressed that I'd ring up his mother and ask her to go in and buy something from him. Some of her best furniture exists as a result of these requests.

A downtown bureaucrat arrived one day and asked to see Jeffrey's secondhand-furniture license, a permit anyone operating an antique store must have. Unaware of this bit of red tape, Jeffrey was so insulted by the terminology "secondhand furniture" that he screamed at the inspector, "I deal in antiques, not secondhand furniture!" and slammed the door on the man's foot as he was trying to flee. I explained to Jeffrey that one needs this kind of licensing, that he had been conducting business for a couple of years without a license, and that to remain in business he would have to go downtown to the Department of Consumer Affairs. From the moment I said this, the idea of a trip downtown never left Jeffrey's brain. He was consumed by the fantasy that he would be arrested and sent away. "I hope I come back today," he said to me the day he built up the nerve to make the trek.

"Don't worry," I told him. "It'll be so stupidly bureaucratic down there that you'll probably be able to survive another two or three years without getting this damned license"—this despite the fact that he practically killed the guy who came to inspect the store.

Five years after Jeffrey began his business, the neighborhood where his store was located, Carnegie Hill, suddenly became very fashionable. And one day he found out that under his new lease, his rent would be doubled. This gave him a very good excuse to close the business, and I know he was relieved to do it.

10. The Takeover

During 1973, there was a worldwide recession, which had a staggering effect on the art market. At auction, many many more lots were failing to meet their reserves. Then, during 1975, in the wake of a slump in overall revenues, the board of directors of Sotheby Parke Bernet decided to go public and floated shares of the company stock on the London stock exchange.

Christie's responded to the recession by introducing the so-called buyer's premium—a 10 percent charge in addition to the hammer price—a practice that was soon after adopted by Sotheby Parke Bernet. And just as the art market began to pick up again, in 1977, Christie's decided to open a New York auction salesroom to go into direct competition with us.

This competition for business between Sotheby Parke Bernet and Christie's had two effects: It propelled the rise of the auction house, which ultimately eclipsed the private gallery to become the most powerful force in the international art world. And Sotheby Parke Bernet, motivated to come up with new schemes to increase our influence as well as our revenues, became a more efficient, better-run company. Heirloom Discovery Days was just one of several new ventures. Another was the establishment of a subsidiary company that would take advantage of the demand for art and furniture restoration.

As the head of decorative arts, I was approached in the late 1970s by John Stair, whose family owned Stair & Company, an English furniture concern. Stair proposed starting a company called Sotheby's Restoration, and together we went to one of Sotheby's financial officers, an executive vice president named Arnold Kagan, with whom we discussed the matter over lunch several times. And Kagan kept saying, "Well, you have to get the business to make money." And I kept saying to Kagan, "We wouldn't be sitting here discussing it if we didn't think we'd get the business and make money."

Needless to say, the idea didn't get very far, until Kagan was about to leave and Fred Schultz was hired in his place. And in 1979, Schultz hired Diana D. Brooks, formerly a loan officer at Citibank, as a financial analyst for Sotheby Parke Bernet. Dede, as she is known, was interested in the restoration company, and within twenty minutes of John Stair's and my first meeting with her, she had put the company together. We were doing business a month later. Today Sotheby's Restoration is still thriving.

Diana Brooks graduated with the first coed class at Yale. Tall and statuesque, she reminds me of Sekhmet, the most powerful lion goddess in the ancient Egyptian pantheon. At Thebes, there's a big alley of Sekhmet statues; over the doorway of Sotheby Parke Bernet in London, coincidentally, there's an ancient Sekhmet head. Shortly after Dede arrived at our offices, she took one look at the books and wisely realized that the equity of the company lies in its expert staff, who have the ability to identify and appraise an object but also possess the well-honed social skills that are needed to deal directly with clients. She understood that the auction world was becoming a specialized, retail market in which the ability to sell is the most important virtue: a good auctioneer is golden; a lousy auctioneer is going to affect the sale in a negative way. When Dede arrived, there was much more of a dichotomy between the art experts and the business people in the company. Experts who got a phone call about prospective business would try to handle the opportunity within their department. Through fostering the idea of teamwork, Dede helped to make the company more efficient and therefore more competitive. By 1986, she was president of Sotheby's North America; and in April 1994, she was made president of Sotheby's Holdings worldwide.

The late seventies–early eighties was a period of expansion for the company, which had more than 2,000 employees worldwide by 1981. In 1980, several million dollars were spent to renovate an office building at York Avenue and Seventy-second Street, which became the home of the decorative arts department. The Madison Avenue branch remained the home of paintings and jewelry. And a space had been rented on East Eighty-fourth Street to accommodate books, stamps, and coins; it was called P.B. 84. By 1982, the costs of running three buildings in New York counteracted a rising volume of sales, and this, in concert with yet another recession in the art market, caused Sotheby Parke Bernet to lose $4.6 million—the first time the company lost money. It was also the first time that Christie's total sales exceeded those of Sotheby Parke Bernet.

In June 1982, our company made an attempt at streamlining. The staff was somewhat downsized, and the Madison Avenue salesroom as well as P.B. 84 and the entire company moved to York Avenue. Rumors were rampant that we were going out of business, and these, in turn, hurt us even more, because they undermined our clients' confidence. Many people who were thinking of selling either held on to their possessions or gave the business to Christie's.

I remember a phone call in December 1982 from a friend who asked if I knew who General Felt was. "What war was he in?" I replied. My friend laughed and explained that General Felt was a carpet company in New Jersey, whose owners, Stephen Swid and Marshall Cogan, also owned Knoll furniture.

Apparently, these two men had slowly been buying shares of Sotheby Parke Bernet on the London exchange; and only after they had purchased 14.2 percent of the company shares did they announce their intention of taking over and reorganizing our floundering company. Swid and Cogan's silent and steady acquisition of shares, though perfectly legal, was seen by the entire staff, particularly by the London office, as the apotheosis of American financial sharks who wanted to "merchandise" Sotheby Parke Bernet. Neither of these men bothered to make overtures toward anyone in the company until their takeover attempt was well underway. Beyond this, Marshall Cogan, formerly an investment broker, had in 1969 been charged with alleged misuse of a client's money. In 1974, he settled out of court with the SEC and agreed to a ban from any further management of discretionary brokerage accounts. Nevertheless, Swid and Cogan saw themselves as bona fide art aficionados, men who collected and who had substantial relationships with both the Metropolitan Museum and the Museum of Modern Art.

In April 1983, Swid and Cogan formally made a $100 million bid to take over our company. The resistance was

1

Whenever I climbed up onto the podium, a hexagonal dais, and just before I began a sale, I felt a strange calm come over me. I felt comfortable up there. I knew that was where I was supposed to be.

Obviously I realized early on how frustrating life can be.

2

4

Geraldine Rockefeller Dodge lived in a gabled, gloomy mansion on an estate called Giralda Farms in New Jersey. After the death of her son, Mrs. Dodge went into complete seclusion—her husband lived in a separate house at the diagonally opposite corner of the property—and devoted the rest of her life to her dogs and to collecting.

When she had her stroke in 1964, there were 186 dogs living in her kennels. A ramp went from the ground floor to her bedroom, and every night eight different dogs would sleep with her.

The tip of the iceberg. When John Marion and I arrived at Giralda, we were overwhelmed by the inventory. There were something close to four thousand bronzes, almost entirely animalier. Mrs. Dodge's obsession for collecting was unlimited and quite simple: If it had an animal on it, she bought it.

The house sale exhibition began on October 4, 1975. Almost ten thousand people a day came through. People were allowed to touch whatever objects were on display; the experience was tactile and intimate.

When I was hired, unhired, and rehired in 1968, Sotheby's Parke Bernet had its galleries in a nondescript building that looked like a limestone sugar cube (above). In 1980, we moved to a much more dramatic space at Seventy-second Street and York Avenue (right).

John L. Marion (far right) and I held a ribbon, while Governor Hugh Carey (center left) and Mayor Edward Koch (center right) did the cutting.

In 1974, the year I was made head of decorative arts at Sotheby's, I had the great good fortune of meeting the love of my life, Jeffrey Childs. Here we are off the coast of Nevis in 1985—before the bad news.

As Jeffrey lay at home dying, I was inextricably committed to preside over a benefit dinner/auction of fifty-six birdhouses designed by some of the most prominent architects in America. This was the first experiment in what would soon become a whole new territory of auctioneering: the ephemera of fantasy objects and privileges that would touch down into the world of acquisition just once and then vanish forever. During the evening, I crossed over an invisible social line and reinvented myself as the auctioneer that everyone has come to know. This birdhouse, designed by Robert A. M. Stern, was bought by Carter Burden for $11,000.

On the morning of one of the sessions, I received a phone call from a client of mine, who said with breathless desperation, "I need some of Andy's cookie jars." It wasn't easy. The moment the auction rounded the bend to the toy section, I handed the gavel over to my colleague David Redden so I could bid on the jars.

12

For the last ten years of his life, Andy Warhol lived in a town house designed by Jed Johnson in an American Federal motif, circa 1820—far removed from the down-town, Factory image of Warhol that one could more readily conjure. After everything was catalogued and 80 percent of what Warhol had collected was removed to the galleries, we conducted private tours for select clients and celebrities as a way of generating even more interest.

13

14

Before the auction, the viewing was quite a scene. All sorts of people, many of whom were visiting the auction house for the first time, poured into Sotheby's. Here is a young collector viewing the infamous cookie jars.

Woolley Walking

15

*Besides becoming a well-known charity auctioneer,
I became what's known in the business as a
"walker," a professional extra man. A lot of people
like to look down on this avocation, but I'd like to
state for the record that it's a very important job
in New York. Though the Walker Handbook of
Etiquette disagrees with me and is predicated
on freebies, my method of being a walker is Dutch
all the way. Even if the husband has already paid
for the tickets, I still like to cover my share.*

*Shortly after Jeffrey died, Mrs. Lawrence
Copley Thaw invited me to the Save
Venice ball. Afterward, the word got out
that I was available, and then the phone
started to ring.*

With Beth de Woody

With Martha Graham

18

With Elizabeth Taylor

19

With Eleanor Lambert

20

With Anne Bass

An amazing combination: Suzanne Bartsch and her husband David Barton surround the late Jerry Zipkin.

Ashton Hawkins escorting Judy Peabody.

Courtesans.

In 1993, I decided to turn my yearly Halloween party into a paid event to benefit Gay Men's Health Crisis, of which I am a board member. Sotheby's agreed to host the event in the main salesroom, though I'm not sure anyone knew what to expect.

With Blaine and Robert Trump.

One of the most prominent realtors in New York, Robby Brown, as Ivana Trump, joined by Jay Gunther.

immediate and bitter. Led by Sotheby Parke Bernet's CEO, Graham Llewellyn, over 110 employees signed a petition saying they would resign should Swid and Cogan gain control. Llewellyn even told one of the British papers, "I'll blow my brains out if they succeed."

Once the takeover bid was official, the board of directors began to search for a white knight who would rescue Sotheby Parke Bernet from what was seen as a couple of parvenus. An overabundance of investment bankers led the search—Warburgs in London, Goldman Sachs in New York—but none of them could come up with anyone. Meanwhile, in March 1983, Lord Westmorland, a member of the Sotheby Parke Bernet board of directors, was in Nassau and happened to run into an acquaintance on the beach. In discussing the plight of the company, he learned of a man named A. Alfred Taubman, of Detroit, who had the kind of money that Sotheby Parke Bernet needed.

Taubman is a real estate developer. In early 1983, along with fellow investors Max Fisher, the retired chairman of United Brands food company, and Henry Ford II, the retired chairman of the Ford Motor Company, Taubman sold a 78,000-acre oceanfront parcel of land in California called the Irvine Ranch for $400 million. These men had purchased the California property in 1977 for a great deal less money, having managed to outbid the Mobil Oil Corporation. Besides being a client of Sotheby Parke Bernet, Taubman was a trustee of the Whitney Museum. In 1980, he had helped the museum raise $1 million to purchase a painting by Jasper Johns.

Westmorland called John Marion to tell him about Taubman, and John Marion in turn contacted one of Taubman's lawyers. Taubman eventually called back and was promptly invited to visit our New York salesroom. Without telling anyone who this man might be, John introduced Taubman around the company and then invited him to attend the March sale of the very important Henry and Louisine Havemeyer collection of Impressionist paintings.

The night of the sale, Graham Llewellyn called John Marion to wish him good luck. It was an important moment. Sotheby's was trying to bounce back from its financial loss of the previous year, and everyone was waiting to see the result of the auction. John Marion told Llewellyn, "Tonight I'm not only selling these paintings. I'm selling the company." He remembers that the atmosphere in the salesroom crackled. The sale was a major success and brought $15 million. And after it was over, Taubman began to make his move.

In the meantime, Swid and Cogan managed to increase their ownership of stock to 29 percent by May 1983. They seemed on the verge of getting the stockholders of Sotheby Parke Bernet to accept their offer, when the British Monopolies and Mergers Commission decided to put a six-month moratorium on the attempted takeover in order to review the bid.

Just after the moratorium was granted, Taubman made a trip to London. He handled Sotheby Parke Bernet's board of directors more gingerly than Swid and Cogan had, giving the impression that he wanted to invest in the company, do some restructuring, but basically leave the running of the business to the experts. His approach was perceived as more gentlemanly, and he received the unanimous blessing of the board of directors to proceed with his bid.

Whereas Swid and Cogan were relying on the resources of three American banks, Taubman's bid was more solid: it was all cash. After some intense negotiations, Taubman, by buying the shares Swid and Cogan had originally purchased, was able to persuade them to withdraw their bid. This gave them a $10 million profit.*

Several months later, Taubman announced that he was the majority shareholder and would have a number of partners, including Henry Ford II and Max Fisher. Against the advice of all his lawyers and financial people, Taubman put up $34 million of his own money against a purchase price of $125 million. At the time, the price seemed exorbitant; now it sounds as though he bought two good Van Goghs. In December 1983, he changed the name of the company back to Sotheby's and appointed Max Fisher as vice chairman. Since then Taubman has realized in excess of $400 million return on his original investment. Although he owns 52 percent of the company's voting shares, he maintains a laissez-faire attitude and leaves the reins of day-to-day control in the able hands of Dede Brooks.

*Which may well have funded their later purchase of the restaurant "21."

11. The Bubble

The worldwide market in Impressionist, modern, and contemporary paintings skyrocketed between 1983 and 1989. A huge amount of wealth had been newly created, and art was the area in which people sought to represent their success. Impressionist and modern art was the most vibrant and identifiable of categories; hung on the wall, it exuded success. And in America particularly, where there was a new breed of aggressive businessman trading in corporate takeovers and real estate speculation and arbitrage, the auction market was seductive. For just as in corporate culture, there was always an underbidder in the art auction. It's reassuring when there is competition to validate your desires, underbidders hitting themselves for failing to win what you won.

In fact, experts agree that the market in these more modern artworks was still reverberating, albeit faintly, from a benchmark sale. In London in 1958, several Impressionist and Postimpressionist paintings belonging to the estate of Jakob Goldschmidt, a German banker who had escaped Hitler and settled in New York City, were auctioned for an unprecedented amount. For example, Paul Mellon bought a Cézanne for over $600,000, twice the amount that had ever been paid for a painting at auction. Obviously, the climate was right for this high-octane bidding, but Erwin Goldschmidt, Jakob's son, had also insisted upon very high reserve prices. And most of them were met. The sense of hard-to-reach exclusivity was only enhanced by the fact that this sale was the first evening event that had ever been held at Sotheby's.

By the mid-1980s, in the early years of Taubman's reign, it had become chic and a bit easier to collect at Sotheby's. The atmosphere was becoming more geared toward the client—in short, more retail. Under Taubman's and Dede Brooks's influence, Sotheby's put an even greater emphasis on financial services and, in fact, created a separate subsidiary in 1984. Sotheby's Financial Services gave the company an ability to lend eminent collectors and dealers money toward the sale or purchase of art at auction.

There were also the Japanese, who had been a major force in art acquisition in the early seventies but then stopped buying when the recession hit America in 1974. During the 1980s, however, real estate values began escalating in Tokyo, which in turn drove up the price of the yen. As a desperate means of controlling these prices, the Japanese began putting arbitrary ceilings on real estate deals. So if you bought a building that was worth $60 million but was ceilinged at $10 million, you had to find a way of selling it and getting your $60 million worth without breaking the law.

One way the Japanese investor got around this was for the prospective buyer of the building to go to the seller and say, "Here's your $10 million. Now, I happen to have a subsidiary company over in America that has a lot of Impressionist pictures. If you take your $10 million and buy $10 million worth of Impressionist pictures from this company, I will buy these

same paintings back from you for $60 million in six months."
Japanese banks trotted right along with the idea, agreeing to
recollateralize $10 million into $60 million. And yet for paintings to be used as collateral, there needs to be a public ex-
pression of their increasing value, and what better way than at
an auction.

Lastly, there was a change in the tax law under President
George Bush in 1986. Suddenly, if a painting in an estate
was worth twenty or thirty times what it was purchased for—
and this, at the time, was not an unreasonable appreciation—
once the law was passed, whoever inherited it could deduct
only the original purchase price upon donation of the painting. This inspired a lot of discretionary selling of artwork, as
opposed to discretionary donation of artwork to museums or
appropriate charities. Organizations such as the British Rail
Pension Fund divested themselves of Impressionist inventory,
as did private collectors such as Douglas Dillon.

And so, under the influence of these three factors, the prices
for many categories of art, but most noticeably Impressionist
and Old Master paintings, rose steeply. Whereas a painting in
either of these categories might have brought one to two million in the early 1980s, Manet's *Rue Mosnier with Street Pavers*
sold for $11 million in 1986; Mantegna's *Adoration of the Magi*
sold for $10.4 million in 1985. Van Gogh's *Sunflowers* was sold
by Christie's to Yasudo Fire & Marine Insurance Company for
$39 million in 1987. Auctions of paintings that normally
brought in a total of $50 million were suddenly bringing in
three times as much. And the bidding unfortunately had nothing to do with aesthetics or passionate involvement; it was all
about the liquidation of money.

During that time, a woman I know brought in an early
Vlaminck, a second-rate Impressionist work she inherited

from her mother, who had acquired it during the fifties for less than $5,000. Despite the fact that the picture was lugubrious, we were able to sell it for $178,000. When a similar Vlaminck came up at auction, it sold for close to $200,000. Obviously, the sale of the first Vlaminck had exerted some influence over the sale of the next Vlaminck that came on the market.

Also during the eighties, a decorator I knew brought in a tiny Renoir—no bigger than four by six inches—of the head of a child. He had received the painting from one of his clients who was having trouble paying his bill. I looked at the painting and commented, "This is a piece of junk; it can't be Renoir." But I checked with the Impressionist department, which located the painting in the catalogue raisonné. However, since it had been cataloged, someone had ambitiously daubed an *R* in the corner of the canvas. I came back to my friend and said, "It's real, all right, but I hope you didn't get taken on it." We affixed an optimistic estimate of $10,000–$15,000, which was far more than I thought the painting was worth. Sotheby's conservation department daubed out the *R*, and in a minor sale during February 1986, this little piece of nothing brought $47,500. I was flabbergasted. I assumed Renoir must've been practically blind when he did it.

Evening sales of that era were truly sought-after events. Tickets to attend them in the main salesroom were hard to acquire, and more clients than ever seemed to be arriving in fur coats and stretch limousines. When a record price was reached in the midst of bidding, a rash of applause would break out in the audience. The most famous and certainly the most controversial Impressionist sale of that era occurred in November 1987, when Van Gogh's *Irises* was sold for $49 million plus premium.

It's interesting to note here that by comparison with all the other Impressionists, Van Gogh's work as a whole consistently brought the highest prices during this boom period. No doubt this was due partly to the notoriety of his mental illness and the story of his self-mutilation (*Irises* was painted when Van Gogh was living in the asylum at Saint-Rémy-de-Provence in the spring of 1889). I like to think that the vibrancy of his technique, which was so much a part of his madness, has now fermented into a kind of accessibility. The sheer intensity of his work seems to reach many more people now than the more muted gentility of painters such as Monet and Renoir.

Irises has had a fascinating provenance. According to Calvin Tomkins, the eminent art critic, it was first the property of Van Gogh's brother, Theo. Exhibited the same year it was painted, it was then stored in an attic room in Montmartre. After Theo's death, it fell into the hands of the man who had supplied Van Gogh with his painting materials, who in turn sold it, in 1892, to the famous French art critic Octave Mirbeau, the first person who had written extensively about Van Gogh's work. Mirbeau in turn sold it, in 1905, to the renowned collector Auguste Pellerin, whose family produced margarine. During the early 1920s, Pellerin sold *Irises* to the Paris art dealer Bernheim-Jeune, who in 1925 sold it to Jacques Doucet, a couturier to the rich and famous, who died shortly thereafter and whose widow sold it to Jacques Seligmann, the owner of a Paris gallery. Seligmann either sold or consigned the painting to a former employees, César de Hauke, who, through a holding company, sold the painting in 1947 for $84,000 to Joan Whitney Payson, the daughter of the financier Payne Whitney.

Joan Payson, a garrulous, large-boned woman, owned the New York Mets and was on the board of trustees of the Metropolitan Museum of Art. Before she died, she asked her children to choose the paintings they wanted, and her son, John, chose *Irises*. He eventually included the painting in the Joan Whitney Payson Gallery of Art, a permanent art collection he established at a small liberal arts college in Maine.

But then the 1986 tax law was passed, which meant that if Payson donated the painting, his deductions would have been limited to the amount his mother paid for it. Beyond this, Van Goghs in general began selling for large amounts of money, and exhibition insurance premiums for *Irises* kept escalating. John Payson put the painting in a vault and approached us about auctioning it.

Once we signed on to auction the painting, we mounted a promotional campaign. *Irises* traveled to several cities in Europe, as well as to Japan. The painting was then exhibited in New York, and for several days before the auction, Sotheby's hosted receptions and a dinner party.

On the unseasonably cold evening of November 11, 1987, traffic was gridlocked on York Avenue as over two thousand people swarmed into Sotheby's to witness the auction. The lot just before *Irises,* Renoir's *Tête de Jeune Fille,* sold to a Japanese collector for $2.3 million. John Marion began the bidding for *Irises* at $15 million, a price that climbed steadily at a million dollars a clip until it reached $31 million. At this point there were only two bidders left: one bidding by telephone through the head of Impressionist and modern painting, David Nash; and the other bidding through our representative Geraldine Nager. The bidding climbed steadily until it reached $49 million, and then the room was frozen in silence. The gavel finally came down.

It was a very important moment. Beyond the fact that it was the highest price ever paid for an Impressionist painting, the sale had taken place less than a month after the October 19,

1987, stock market crash. Ultimately, the sale of *Irises* was cited as a proof that artworks were immune to the current economic crises.

All that anyone knew about the person who bought *Irises* was that he was supposedly an overseas buyer. But two years after the sale, it was learned that Alan Bond, an Australian beer brewer of flagrant wealth, was the surreptitious purchaser. Bond was already well known for having led an Australian yachting team to victory in the America's Cup, the first time the Cup was ever taken away from America.

Alan Bond had seen *Irises* at its New York exhibition in November 1987 and fallen in love with it. Most art historians were in agreement that in comparison to other Van Goghs that had recently come up for sale, the coloration of *Irises* was noticeably more vibrant. Bond, who had bought art through Sotheby's on previous occasions, spoke to us about borrowing against the purchase price under the condition that he put up *Irises* as well as some of his other valuable paintings as collateral. A repayment arrangement was arranged, and Mr. Bond bought the painting for $53.9 million.

Two years later, after having made several amortized payments, Bond announced that he had borrowed from Sotheby's to buy *Irises*. Once it was learned that we had financed the sale, a lot of criticism was flung at the company, basically for having possibly manipulated the price with the prospect of a loan. People were also upset on a philosophical level, because the price had been cited as a benchmark for subsequent art auctions. So not only were we accused of manipulating the price; we were also accused of manipulating the market. The way I looked at the situation, it was hardly different from a bank lending money for the purchase of expensive real estate. It was just like a mortgage.

It all might have blown over had Mr. Bond not gotten into financial trouble, causing us to threaten foreclosure of the loan. We were eventually able to negotiate a sale of *Irises* to the Getty Museum; a confidentiality pledge was signed by Dede Brooks and several principals at the Getty, and the purchase price was kept a tight secret, even from me. But I assume the painting went for more than $60 million. It was a long haul, but we made money in the end.

The height of the Impressionist market and the highest volume of any one sale at Sotheby's occurred in May 1989, when we auctioned $469 million worth of paintings in a single evening sale. Manet's *Walk,* owned by Alan Bond, was sold to a Japanese bidder for $14.9 million and went toward the repayment of Bond's loan. Now, during the mid-1990s, if we have an Impressionist sale that brings $25 to $35 million, it's considered a triumph.

Today Sumitomo Bank of Japan owns more than seven thousand Impressionist pictures that sit in their vaults, listed on the books for more than $6 billion. They avoid putting them up for auction because the moment one painting brings a lot less than what they paid for it, then the whole collection will have to be reappraised. The pictures might be worth a billion or a billion and a half now.

In 1989, the gross sales of Sotheby's in New York was $1.5 billion (worldwide sales were $3 billion), and the profit margin was $113 million. The gross receipts of selling six thousand pictures reached $1.2 billion. The remaining $300 million was generated from my part of the company, decorative arts, in 66,000 lots. At the time, I used to joke that the painting divisions were making all the money while we, in decorative arts, were doing all the work. After all, we dealt with ten times the number of lots for a quarter of the money.

Decorative arts has always been the core business at Sotheby's. It's the bread and butter, it's what attracts more people to work as dealers or in auction houses than any other category. Not everybody can afford to put millions of dollars on a wall, but they might have $5,000 for a nice Georgian chair. During the Impressionist frenzy, the decorative arts became the poor stepchildren of Sotheby's departments. If the painting department needed fifteen people to catalog two pictures, they got them. Whereas in an area such as porcelain—which handles three thousand lots a year—Letitia Roberts, the department head and an employee for more than twenty-five years, worked with one assistant and often came in seven days a week. But then, during the early nineties, the real estate crunch in Tokyo eased up, the Japanese buyers all but disappeared, and discretionary selling pretty much ceased. When sales of Impressionist works of art began to bring only $15–$20 million, my decorative arts were still doing $300 million.

And yet as a result of the plummeting Impressionist market, other departments at Sotheby's had a more difficult time maintaining business. Even the somewhat sophisticated public harbored the feeling that if an Impressionist painting couldn't be sold for a stupid amount of money, then there was no point in selling anything else. My response was, "Well, maybe your Renoir is worth a lot less, but your Georgian dining table is worth a lot more, and so is your Georgian silver. Your Fabergé, however, is just the same."

12. Birds in Flight

As typically happens in New York City, two dogs sniff each other's butts and the course of your life is changed forever. My black Lhasa apso, Hank, met a white Lhasa called Tarzan on Ninety-sixth Street. And after I had chatted with Tarzan's owner, Dr. Raschbaum, we decided to breed Hank to Tarzan's mother, whose name was Bella, the next time she went into heat.

Six months later, I received a phone call from someone with a very distinctive voice. There was no introduction, no salutation, just "Bring over your cat."

"I don't have a cat. Who is this, please?"

"This is Dr. Raschbaum."

"I remember you. But we never discussed cats. We only talked dogs. I have a Lhasa named Hank."

"Oh, that's right. Well, then I'm going to give you Bella."

This was my second conversation with the man, and he was giving me his dog—one I had never seen. I was understandably reticent. "Well, you know, we've only really met once. I would think you'd want to interview me and let me interview your dog before you give her to me."

He asked me to stop by as soon as possible.

A half hour later, I was walking into the apartment, and the moment I rounded the corner, Bella came screaming over to me and chomped me on the ankle. Suddenly I didn't think owning her was such a good idea. Tarzan, however, greeted me in a much more civilized manner, and I said to Dr. Raschbaum, or Bill, as he admonished me to call him, "What about the puppy?"

The puppy, as it turned out, was his favorite of Bella's litter, which included Atlas, Hercules, and Amazonia. He apologized for having me come to his apartment, but he couldn't possibly part with Tarzan.

"Well, I'm a little wary of Bella because, after all, she just bit me."

"That's understandable," said Bill.

Two weeks later, the phone rang and it was Dr. Raschbaum. "Okay, come and get Tarzan." I was thrilled, because now I'd have a black Lhasa and a white Lhasa, which would be like a Tibetan version of Black & White Scotch. When I arrived, I noticed a lot of packing boxes. And I said, "Are you moving?"

Bill and his wife, Mary, had leased a town house on the West Side. They were both doctors—he was a gynecologist, she was a psychologist—and they wanted to practice where they lived. He happened to mention as an aside that they were having trouble renting out their current apartment, which was at Ninety-sixth and Fifth, right on Central Park. In fact, he had until the following day to find a sublessee. The rent was $1,000, which was rather hefty back in 1976; it was $400 more than Jeffrey and I were paying for our two apartments at 12 East 97th Street.

Whenever Jeffrey and I had discussed living together, his one caveat was that he didn't want to give up any of the rooms we already had separately. Knowing that it would be difficult to find an affordable apartment with four bedrooms and four bathrooms, I realized that this was his way to avoid taking the next step in the relationship: living together. As it turned out, the Raschbaums' flat had more rooms than our apartments combined.

I arrived home from work at eight that evening, described to Jeffrey the glorious apartment I'd seen, and informed him that we had until the following morning to decide whether or not we wanted it. Jeffrey, who hated the idea of being up-rooted, was not very happy. He put up all kinds of lame arguments against moving. I endured his sophistry for as as long as I could, then got so frustrated that I punched a hole in my kitchen's plasterboard wall. That broke the spell of contention. We went to see the place at nine o'clock the next morning, and by nine-ten, Jeffrey was saying that if we didn't get the apartment, he'd do something drastic.

Shortly after we moved into 1150 Fifth Avenue, Jeffrey went down to New Orleans and came back with a mealy green Amazonian parrot. He wanted to name it Woolley, but I thought that would be too confusing, so I suggested he give it my middle name, which is Carleton. We kept Carleton in the sunny bedroom that faced the northwest corner of Fifth Avenue. I could never use it, because I love to sleep late in the dark. Jeffrey and I decided to turn this room into our aviary.

Many years before, Sotheby's had gaveled the estate of Reba Rubin, who lived at 993 Fifth Avenue. Her boudoir and bedroom were covered in beveled four-inch-wide mirrored strips. The Citibank representative who had charge of the apartment said it could never be sold with all those mirrored panels, so I offered to take them away and have the bedroom painted. Only after I had them peeled from the walls did I discover that they were marked "Baccarat, Made in France." At the time, I had no place for them, but I knew I would have a place one day, so they had remained in my closet for some years. Jeffrey and I decided to use the strips as decoration in the aviary—around doorways, moldings, baseboards, the sides of the cage, pretty much as they had been used before.*

The aviary was a great wooden cage that was fifteen feet long, six feet deep, and ceiling high. And after we finished building it, we gradually assembled a menagerie of almost one hundred fifty birds. Jeffrey had an avian obsession and loved to patronize pet shops. One day he came home with a piebald jay from Central America in a shoe-box cage. It was as big as a crow, with black and white plumage on its body and a rash of blue feathers over the eyes, with a yellow and black spot in the middle of the cluster. For some reason, its tail was missing. The bird was eerie-looking, to say the least.

When I put the new jay into the cage, I saw all of the hundred and fifty other birds cram themselves against the south side of the enclosure. This had never happened before. I went to get the bird book and looked up piebald jays. I read: "This large aggressive bird should not be caged with little birds." By the time I had finished reading, the jay had stalked one of the spice finches and was devouring it. So we had to move the jay out of the big cage and into another cage in the room. We started calling him Killer. It wasn't that Killer was evil; after all,

*Later on, during the mid-eighties, on page 386 of a biography of Elsie de Wolfe, there was mention of the mirrored bedroom and bath that the famous decorator had done for Mrs. Rubin. From then on, the room became the Elsie de Wolfe Aviary, because it was almost a replica of what I had taken from the Rubin apartment. For a long time, I used to kid everyone and say that Elsie de Wolfe had done the decorating here.

eating other birds was his nature. He was otherwise a very pleasant pet.

On the advice of Jeffrey's cousin, who worked at the Bronx Zoo, we used to feed Killer a carrotburger filled with crushed eggshell. I made that for him every day for seventeen years. Once the other birds got wind of the fact that Killer was receiving custom-made food, they began clamoring for carrotburgers too. Killer also thrived on mealworms. Twenty thousand of them were mailed to us every two weeks from a company in Ohio.

I used to let Killer out of his cage, and he'd fly around the room until I snapped my fingers, whereupon he'd go back in. Later on, I acquired some Lady Gould finches, which are very colorful, and I put a bunch of them in Killer's cage, on the other side of a partition. On Killer's side of the cage we placed Rufus, a blue and gold macaw, and Carleton, our original Amazonian parrot, who years later put out one of Killer's eyes, thus giving him his comeuppance for offing the finch. Claiborne, the red-billed hornbill, was the only big bird I was able to trust with the finches. I also had a cockatoo—as well as a red conure, who eat only fruit. When the aviary was at its height of productivity, we had five or six diets going. It was a nightmare to contend with on a daily basis, but I loved it.

In its heyday, the aviary was a much-talked-about venue in New York, a glorious attraction for many people who visited us. Once, a friend of mine came by for dinner and looked into the aviary and wanted to know where the windows faced. When I told her they overlooked Central Park, she said, "My God, I just spent five million dollars on an apartment on Fifth Avenue so I could have a view of the park, and you gave yours to the birds."

The aviary became a great reference point in our lives; the room on Fifth Avenue was one of the first places friends would visit when they came up to the apartment. Having such a profusion of life in the apartment was uplifting, and on weekend nights when Jeffrey would go off on his downtown exploits, I would sometimes sit in the aviary room and read and listen to the nocturnal stirrings of our great brood.

⸎

The early eighties were when we began to hear about the strange plague that was afflicting gay men. We learned of people who were getting sick; then the illness began to strike people we knew. In an effort to face what was happening, Jeffrey and I ordered brochures from Gay Men's Health Crisis. Once, Jeffrey said to me, "If anybody should have AIDS, it should be me."

"It's not a matter of being gay or what you might have done," I insisted. "Nobody should have this disease. It's one of life's great tragedies that it even exists."

In 1986, a brochure that came in the mail described weight loss and thrush. Reading it, I began to worry, because Jeffrey had lost weight and had had a white rash in his mouth. He tended to be paunchy, and slimming down had made him a bit more egotistical. I remember someone saying to him around that time, "You must have lost twenty pounds." "Yeah," he said. "I now have my weight under control. I look great, don't I? And I don't have AIDS."

I pushed these thoughts away until one night just before Christmas. I was trimming the tree, and I went into the bedroom for a pair of scissors and noticed Jeffrey sleeping. Although he was only forty, he had this old look about him. I knew then that he was probably sick, and I sat down and cried. The next morning, I made a doctor's appointment for the day after Christmas. And when I told Jeffrey what I had done, he stared back at me with a look of horror on his face. He couldn't deny it anymore.

By the time we went to the doctor, Jeffrey was already suffering from shortness of breath. We were about to travel to Saint Kitts for ten days and were concerned about being so far from our medical lifelines. But the doctor gave Jeffrey Bactrim and told us to take our trip if we wanted to.

The plane ride certainly didn't improve Jeffrey's symptoms, and they worsened while we were on the island. It was strange to have his illness looming over our heads in such an Eden-like place. He declined so rapidly that he was soon unable to walk two feet without feeling tired. In fact, he slept most of the time, while I wondered what the next part of our life was going to be like. One day the Caribbean was incredibly warm, something like eighty-five degrees, and Jeffrey decided he was going to attempt a short swim. The moment he submerged himself, he was stricken with a terrible chill. Five days into the trip, we looked at each other and said, "We've got to get out of here."

I remember flying over the dense green jungles of Saint Kitts, the pristine beaches and the languid palm trees, and thinking how beautiful it was down there and how strange my life was becoming. I took Jeffrey to the hospital right from the airport, and he was diagnosed with pneumocystis carinii pneumonia, the opportunistic infection that claimed and killed the majority of AIDS patients in 1986.

Jeffrey was in the hospital for several weeks, infused with intravenous treatments. When he came home, he had aged a great deal more and his body was wasting rapidly. And he just kept aging and wasting. Every month, he seemed to grow ten years older. That last period of his life, from Christmas of 1986 until July 4, 1987, seemed like forever at the time. Now it seems like a hiccup.

When someone you love is dying, the world can take on a paradoxical tint. Jeffrey and I were collectors of a certain kind of porcelain service called Barr Flight. We had almost the whole service, but we were missing the Holy Grail of the set, the teapot. One afternoon in early May 1987, just before Jeffrey's forty-first birthday on the eighteenth, I stopped by a local antique shop on my way home from visiting him in the hospital. Jeffrey had spent a great deal of money in this shop over the years. When I walked in and saw the teapot, I asked the proprietor, who knew that Jeffrey and I were collectors of this design, why she hadn't told him about it. She said the teapot had literally just come in.

Going to visit him on his birthday, I had a wrapped package with me. Jeffrey grinned at me from his bed and said intuitively, "You found my teapot." When I nodded, he seemed uproariously pleased, and we sat there chatting about my great find. It was one of the few moments of release during that time. It was also the last real conversation we ever had. Jeffrey was suffering from toxoplasmosis, which affects the brain, not to mention coordination and speech, and from that point onward he was out of it for most of the time. He remained in the hospital until early June, at which point he said he was so depressed that he just wanted to come home. But then, after three days at home, he announced that he wished to be dead. It was a very painful moment for me, because I wasn't ready to let go of him. And knowing how difficult he could be, I turned to him and said, "Jeffrey, that's very hard for me to hear. So if you have nothing else to say other than that, please don't say anything." After that he said very little.

It was like watching one of those hand-wound phonograph players slowly running out. There was no *sturm und drang*. I watched his body waste away, and by the time he died, he wasn't here at all. The brain fever had plagued him into dullness. And in a way that was fortunate, because it would have been a lot worse had he known fully what was happening to him.

Now I say that if my life becomes inexorably bad, if I catch some insidious disease that is beyond fixing or coping with or ameliorating, I'd like to be able to commit suicide, not out of desperation but as a friendly act to avoid going through all of those inevitable and agonizing stages of dying.

"They'll find something," people tell me optimistically. "You wait and see, Robert. Something will break." But I understand enough about AIDS and its various complications to know that finding one thing to change the tide of dying will not just happen.

I inherited many things from Jeffrey, but one of the most sentimental of his bequests to me was the jadeite bear that on our first date he'd mistakenly told me was made by Fabergé. I'm glad I didn't hold it against him. As it turned out, he wasn't the only one who thought the bear was Fabergé. Several years after he died, I met his jadeite bear's doppelgänger at the New York Antique Show. It was being offered by Kenneth Snowman, of Wartski's of London, the only person in the world besides the Schaffers of A La Vieille Russie who deals mainly in Fabergé. When I noticed what looked like an exact replica of Jeffrey's jadeite bear for sale for $28,000, I went home and returned the next day with Jeffrey's bear in my pocket. I asked Snowman if I could look at his bear, and he brought it out. Then, to distract him, I asked a pertinent question about an object in another corner of the booth and managed to place Jeffrey's bear next to his without his seeing. They were identical, from the arch of the back to the setting of the feet to the diamond eyes. Finally, I indicated what I'd done. "So which is yours?" I asked. He was flabbergasted. He couldn't tell them apart.

"Is yours Fabergé?"

"Oh yes, quite, quite," he said.

"Well, mine isn't. It was bought nearly thirty years ago for four hundred fifty dollars and was made by the Imperial Lapidary Works during the Fabergé era. But it is not Fabergé. So then, which is which?" I asked one of the two experts on Fabergé in the world.

He couldn't tell me, other than that his was priced at $28,000.

When I went to Peter Schaffer, the other expert, and told him, he said that they couldn't be identical.

"Trust me," I said. "I can tell whether these things are identical or not." I knew my bear was not Fabergé. The dealer's jadeite bear was an exact replica of mine. If he wanted to sell it as Fabergé, that was up to him.

In a sense, I also inherited our aviary. It continued to thrive until two years ago. While I was in Venice, there was a bad storm in New York with very strong winds, and one of the windows that had been incorporated into the Elsie de Wolfe Aviary blew out. Half of the little birds decided to leave—the African weavers, mostly. They just made a beeline for Central Park, and I haven't seen them since.

I had always been nonchalant about the birds and their varied lives and deaths, but when I heard that one of the big ones, Claiborne, the red-billed hornbill, had also flown away, I was upset. But by the time I returned from Venice, Claiborne had magically come back. His saga was pretty unbelievable.

Claiborne had flown out with the other birds, landed in Central Park, and was picked up by homeless man, who sold him for twenty dollars to a construction worker, who was renovating a town house on Ninety-fifth Street.

In the meantime, a friend had gone around to pet shops within a ten-block radius and left the bird's description, with my name and phone number. The construction worker brought Claiborne to his home in New Jersey and tried to feed him birdseed, but Claiborne ate only worms, mixed fruits, and the famous mix of hamburger and carrot. After three days, the man went to a pet store near his job and asked what he should feed an exotic bird he had found. The shop owner asked the appropriate questions, and when he realized that the bird in question might be Claiborne, he took the construction worker's name and got in touch with me. A few days later, on a Saturday afternoon, the man arrived with his son to visit the aviary. And when he returned Claiborne, I gave him $100 as a reward.

⟪ ⟫

In 1994, I found out that my T-cell count had dropped to 46. There were too many diseases that I was at risk of catching from the birds. I was most concerned that Jeffrey's and my birds have a good home, particularly Rufus, the blue and gold macaw. Macaws can live for quite a long time, sometimes as long as a century, and Rufus was only two years old when Jeffrey and I bought him in 1976. I once met a man who had met King George III's macaw. George III died in 1820, and the bird died in 1906.

I gave the little birds who were left to a friend of a friend. Claiborne and the four other big ones now live with the painter Hunt Slonum, who has one hundred twenty exotic birds in his aviary on Houston Street. Hunt got $6,000 worth of birds, for which he appropriately traded one of his bird paintings. It now hangs in the same room the aviary was in. I later learned that Claiborne is a female red-billed hornbill— Hunt had raised two males and was able to identify her sex. Shortly before she flew the coop the first time, Carleton, the homicidal parrot, had been chasing her. At least she doesn't have to worry about him anymore. The rest of her life should be ideal.

Three weeks from the day that the last of the birds left, I had to give a rehearsal dinner for Mayor Giuliani's chief of staff, who was getting married the next day. It was a large affair, which made it necessary for me to use the aviary room. The problem was that the parrots had chewed the wood frame on the windows all the way through to the brick. It was a total mess. All the cages needed to be dismantled, the glass strips preserved and stored, the walls papered, and new carpeting installed. Throughout that whole three weeks, I kept telling the laborers involved that the work had to be completed because the mayor was coming for dinner. Luckily, they finished in time.

13. Andy and a Bit of Lee

Andy Warhol had a black belt in shopping; he was the ultimate accumulator. All through his life he could be completely smitten—if only for a few fleeting moments—by some object, which he'd buy and never look at again. His famous-for-fifteen-minutes philosophy certainly expressed itself in his personal shopping style. Warhol was merely an acquaintance of mine; he did a lot of auction buying at Sotheby's, and we often passed each other in the tight nightly orbit of New York's social functions. The great irony of Andy's life is that he died in his late fifties under the care of a nurse who may have had a lapse in attention. I was somewhat better acquainted with his former lover Jed Johnson, as well as with Fred Hughes, the editor of *Interview* magazine and Andy's best friend and business partner. I had met them through mutual contacts among the velvet mafia, the network of prominent and successful gay men and women who are publicly out. My connections within that sphere helped to influence the Warhol Estate and particularly its executor, Fred Hughes, to choose Sotheby's to handle Warhol's acquisitions. His inventory was so vast and voluminous that out of our thirty-eight departments, the only one that didn't catalog any of his possessions was Judaica.

As it turned out, the Warhol and the Liberace estates came to the block within the same month, April 1988. In 1987, shortly after Liberace died, I flew out to the West Coast, where I was given a whirlwind tour of the entertainer's penthouse on Sunset Boulevard, his house on the beach in Malibu, his grand house in Palm Springs, and three tract homes in a development in Las Vegas. There was also a house at Lake Tahoe, which I never got to.

The fact that Liberace died of AIDS is spoken of now, but at the time it was one of those "anything but" explanations. Which sounds as ridiculous as the contention that he wasn't gay. When one thinks of Liberace's high exposure and money, it would seem that he—like Andy Warhol—could at least put together a very interesting collection of objects. But the essence of Liberace was primarily what I call *gold-plated silver plate*, of which there were probably twenty thousand pieces in his collection. Silver plate in and of itself brings in only two figures per item, unless, of course, it's Sheffield and early nineteenth century—which is *not* what Liberace's was—and then it might be worth three figures per item. Gold plating doesn't enhance value at all. Liberace was characterized by a quirky decorator leitmotif: he had a place to eat in every room of every house, excluding the bedrooms and bathrooms. There would be a table with six to twelve place settings, including napkins and water glasses, each with its own peculiar color scheme. I was told that the settings were changed with some regularity. The twenty thousand pieces of gold-plated silver plate were acquired to deal with all these tables.

I assume the general idea was: I'm bringing friends over, let's eat in this room, it's already set up. Obviously, some people in this world think it's impressive to have a table set up and ready for dining whenever you walk from one room to the next. But I didn't catch on to this right away. And the first time I visited the Los Angeles residences—Malibu and Sunset Boulevard—I kept asking, "Were people coming to dinner all the time with this man?"

"Oh, no, that was just his way of *displaying*," I was told.

I wandered around, trying desperately to find objects that had some real value. I don't want to sound blasé; I was actually dying to do the Liberace sale. My grandmother was one of those devoted ladies who, every Wednesday night come hell or high water, was in front of the television, watching the great man and his brother George. I would have thought that at least the candelabrum on top of his piano would be solid silver; but no, it too was plated, like everything else.

Las Vegas was Liberace's main base. He had bought three tract houses, connected them together, and aggrandized their modesty in a way that I'd never seen done before. According to his sister and his housekeeper, the reason Liberace had made such a middle-class purchase was that he never wanted to lose touch with "the people." And this house certainly was a contrast to Wayne Newton's nearby "Casa Shenandoah," a 150-acre estate full of exotic birds and Arabian horses. From the outside, Liberace's casa looked like the annex of a trailer park.

Inside, it was very Louis XVI, or I should say, reproduction Louis Louis. There was a picture of his mother in every room—a very Greek Orthodox touch, though Liberace was not Greek Orthodox. The master bathroom had a sunken circular bathtub with columns all around, and up on the ceiling was a painting of Liberace in mauve, gazing down from the clouds. "What are we going to see next," I said, "the Sistine Chapel?"

And then we went into his bedroom, and there it was, the Sistine Chapel frescoes reproduced on a ceiling that was only eight and a half feet high. If you were tall enough, you could touch God touching man. I'd never seen anything like it.

That was the moment when I conceived a brilliant marketing strategy: make every blue-hair in America who still loved Liberace feel compelled to get on a bus from Chicago, Saint Louis, or wherever and go to Las Vegas; take out advertisements to let everyone know that a piece of Liberace's silver plate could be had for $400; and for that $400 we'd throw in a house tour, a catalog, and a certificate of authenticity.

I wanted to hire out half the convention center in Las Vegas on Memorial Day weekend, which is traditionally a very dry weekend for gambling. I knew I could get a good deal on the space. We needed room to display everything—we were looking at literally thousands of things. I wanted to put together a hardbound catalog for $29.95 to be sold on television—CNN was my original thought—and have commercials running that said, "Call Atlanta. You, too, can have the Liberace sale." My marketing plan may sound a bit over the top, and yet with hindsight I know I had the right instinct to maximize the collection, making a silk purse out of a sow's ear.

I went to Liberace's executor/lawyer and said there would be at least a million dollars' worth of expenses by the time we'd printed up the catalog and then advertised the sale on television. I figured that we'd make two million dollars on the catalog before even conducting the auction. I wanted to pack up the inventory in all his homes in Los Angeles and Palm Springs and ship everything to Las Vegas, where it would be sold in a high-pitched auction. I told the executor that if I was going to go to all this trouble, I wanted a media event, which would make a lot of money. I said to him, "I want a carrot out there, not a stick. I want to orchestrate a beautiful exhibition and a nutsy auction, and for that you're going to pay me appropriately."

Christie's took a very different approach. They came in cheap and simple, with a standard commission rate of 10 percent of the gross sale. They proposed to go into partnership with Butterfield and Butterfield, an auction house on the West Coast, and their offer was ultimately accepted.

After I received the news that Sotheby's had been rejected, I went into Diana Brooks's office and said, "Dede, I've got good news and I've got bad news."

"What's the bad news?"

"Christie's got Liberace."

"So what's the good news?"

"*We* don't have to do Liberace."

Christie's ended up putting all of Liberace's belongings on racks and tables in a convention center in an out-of-the-way part of Los Angeles. Whereas the Liberace sale brought only $2 million, Warhol was auctioned the same month in our more flamboyant style and made $25 million.

◖◖ ◗◗

The difference between Liberace and Warhol was that Liberace had a lot of taste, mostly bad, whereas Warhol had taste that was unusually prescient and wonderful and, at its worst, still quirky and interesting. When you looked at Warhol's things you'd say either, "Well, it's weird, but I like it," or "It's exquisite, it's very high quality." Only rarely did you come across something banal or prosaic, unless of course you hate Fiesta ware. Even so, you couldn't help but be impressed by how much Fiesta ware Warhol had. People used Fiesta ware—

dazzling-colored plates that weren't considered at all precious in the 1930s and '40s and '50s—as everyday service, and after the plates became scratched, they were thrown away. It was a compelling mystery why Warhol accumulated the volume that he did.

Andy Warhol was a mild-mannered Slovak from Pittsburgh, who began as a window dresser at Bergdorf's and did drawings of shoes. He became a legend in his own mind and reinvented himself more than a few times. Pop Art as it was understood by the masses was made possible by Andy Warhol, who became its grand iconographer as well as its icon. And yet Warhol himself had enough cynical self-knowledge to appreciate how silly and serendipitous his vaunted stature was. I think he was greatly amused by the clamor.

One reason I respect his art is that he was so straightforward about it. If someone asked Warhol when he painted a certain image, he would often respond, "I'm not sure I did. It was done at the Factory." The fact that he could admit this means he had a great deal of confidence and style. His first works from the fifties and early sixties, which include some of the Campbell's Soup Cans and the Brillo Boxes and the shoes and illustrations for windows, are in the strictest sense the true autographed Warhols.

Warhol was really the person who transformed the multiple print and made the idea of owning one as desirable as and sometimes even more desirable than owning an original, unduplicated painting. It was a very important moment in contemporary art history when a Campbell's Soup Can brought the famous price of $60,000 in 1969 at a Sotheby Parke Bernet auction. Whether or not Warhol actually painted it was not the point. In a sense, the *artist* became the object of the bidding, and the specific work was secondary. This was only enhanced by Warhol's quirky personality, his exotic habits, the fact that he was, for the most part, completely laconic.

◖◗

We found out later that there was a relationship between the person who consigned that landmark Campbell's Soup Can to us and the person who bought it for $60,000. The consignor, who was Swiss, wanted the price to go up as high as it did, presumably, to inflate the value of forthcoming Warhol inventory. Such practices go on constantly, a consignor using an auction house for his own shilling operation. A public price realized at auction enhances the value of the artist's inventory and naturally carries a lot more influence than a comparable price received by a private art gallery. And yet as long as the bill and the commissions are paid, we would have absolutely no way of knowing about such a precooked scheme.

Still, determining price remains difficult, especially if there are taxes involved—i.e., capital gains tax for sellers, estate taxes for estates. The IRS defines fair market value as the price realized between a willing seller and a willing buyer, all facts, such as condition, origin, and autograph, known publicly. A lot of dealers lament that at Sotheby's, sales tend to get a great deal of media attention, which drives up the prices (it certainly was to be one of the complaints surrounding the Warhol sale). But if a journalist went to ask a dealer what he sold during any given week and for how much, the journalist would be told it was none of his business.

At a Christie's auction in 1989, over $4 million was paid for *Shot Red Marilyn,* which more recently was re-auctioned in 1994 for $3.6 million. Although whoever purchased Marilyn at $4 million lost a little bit of money, the fact that she was still worth many millions is a great coup for the work of Warhol. One great reason why the Warhols are still considered valuable, I believe, is that they are so completely recognizable, even from a hovering helicopter.

The Andy Warhol I knew was a terse man, who used the word "great" to describe everything he saw. My whole view of him changed one evening in Hong Kong in 1984. There was a very la-di-da supper club—created in one of the city's new buildings—whose members were exclusively Chinese billionaires. I had been invited to dinner along with six other people, including Warhol and Fred Hughes. Andy and Fred had brought over several dozen Warhols to decorate the club for its grand opening. These paintings were, of course, available for purchase.

At one point during the dinner, Andy started to hold forth about art, specifically his view of twentieth-century art vis-à-vis the traditions of the nineteenth century. Then he began to speak about Hong Kong, its political situation, its relationship with China, its place in the modern world. From the monosyllabic mutterer, he was transformed into this highly articulate, cultured-sounding man.

After spending that evening with Warhol in Hong Kong, I came to realize that in many ways Andy Warhol truly enjoyed himself.

For the last ten years of his life, Warhol lived in a town house on Sixty-sixth Street between Park and Madison; the interior was designed by his longtime companion, Jed Johnson. Jed had elegant taste, very different from the style with which Warhol is associated. The house itself was done in an American Federal motif, circa 1820. Friezes on the walls were neoclassical, and the walls themselves were glazed—all in all, far removed from the "downtown," "Factory" image of Andy Warhol that one could more readily conjure. According to Fred Hughes, when Warhol was gearing up to move into the town house, he was, on one hand, horrified at the idea of appearing conventional or grand, and yet, at the same time, he loved the luxury of his new environment.

The town house was completed in 1974. Warhol proceeded to move in, and only a few years later, his relationship with Johnson dissolved and Johnson moved out, and Warhol had free rein to clutter the house with his possessions.

Warhol liked to be picked up at ten-thirty in the morning. Then he would shop himself into a stupor. He'd come to auctions, go antiquing, visit the Jewelry Exchange on Forty-seventh Street. He could breeze into a store, spy a certain bracelet, ask how much it weighed, and then tell the salesman he wanted to shave a bit off the price because the bracelet was encumbered by a topaz. He got away with it. And when he arrived back at the house, he usually left whatever he'd just bought in the bag, put it down somewhere and forgot about it.

By the time Sotheby's representatives came to the town house in 1987, we could barely open the dining room doors. The enormous space was chock-full, floor to ceiling, of wrapped stuff. It took us almost three months to unwrap Warhol and figure out what everything was and where it should go. And that was just for one room. Andy loved the sport of acquisition. He had a very good eye but no limit to his themes.

Although we organized the sale of Warhol's private collection of paintings by, among others, Picasso, Edvard Munch, Cy Twombly, Robert Rauschenberg, Jasper Johns, Marcel

Duchamp, Roy Lichtenstein, and the newcomer Jean-Michel Basquiat, the large inventory of Warhol's own work was retained by the estate.

In addition to the paintings, we cataloged all sorts of objects that had been acquired by Warhol and left to pile up in his house. Some of the highlights of this voluminous cataloging were 175 cookie jars, an incredible collection of Art Deco and Art Nouveau objects and furnishings, a bag full of high school graduation rings, boxes upon boxes of Fiesta ware, World War II medals, toy soldiers, and Eskimo masks. There was a lot of American Federal furniture and decorations, including nineteenth-century beds, flatware, tea sets, and tables. There were Indian artifacts, including Navajo blankets, jewelry, and tomahawks, and many more fanciful items, such as Miss Piggy beach towels and space toys. There were bags of gold coins, gold and silver bullion.

While we were in the midst of inventorying the town house, Warhol's friend Suzie Frankfurt kept ringing me up.

"How's the jewelry?" she'd say.

"We haven't found any jewelry."

"That's impossible. I spent years with him buying jewelry on Forty-seventh Street. It's got to be there."

"Well, we're still at it, but nothing so far."

These repeated phone calls were rather demoralizing: we couldn't find this hidden cache anywhere. After yet another one of Suzie Frankfurt's calls, I resorted to phoning Fred Hughes, figuring that Andy Warhol's best friend and alter ego would know something. Fred said he wasn't sure if Warhol had kept the jewelry or not. Andy Warhol appeared to have been inscrutable even to his inner circle. We had no choice but to keep on emptying the house and doing our inventory. Still we came up with nothing.

One afternoon, when we were in the middle of photographing Warhol's bedroom for the catalog, the photogra-
pher needed to get a better angle on the Georgian mahogany
four-poster bed. But when the porters went to move the bed,
they couldn't budge it. It was weighed down by something
substantially heavy. Warhol's four-poster had a rather sturdy
canopy on top. When one of the porters stood on a stool and
tried to dismantle the tester, all the missing jewelry turned up.
It seems that every time Andy came home with a newly acquired piece of jewelry, he'd give it a toss up to the canopy.
Rather than wear it, he slept under it. And nobody in Andy's
life seemed to know. That's how furtive he was. On its own,
the jewelry brought a little more than $3 million.

After everything was cataloged and 80 percent of what
Warhol had collected was removed to the galleries, we smart-
ened up the town house with Jed Johnson's help and got it
looking the way it was in 1974, before Andy moved in. Private tours for select clients and celebrities would, we felt, be
a way of generating even more interest. A lot of people were
fascinated by Warhol and by the idea that he had amassed such
an eclectic range of possessions. I personally took Tommy Tune
through, as well as Jerome Zipkin, who in 1987 was still playing his role of social consort to Nancy Reagan. We then threw
a few private dinner parties, and the press office was besieged
by requests from well-connected people who wanted to be invited. And once the dishes were cleared from the last dinner
party at Warhol's town house, the rest of the artist's possessions
were moved to the salesroom at Sotheby's.

Even before the auction, the viewing was quite a scene. All
sorts of people, many of whom were visiting the auction
house for the first time, poured into Sotheby's; and the steady
stream of mostly curiosity-seekers never abated until the last

of the sales were over. Indeed, the sixteen-session sale of Warhol's estate was mobbed with people who believed their lives would be enhanced by owning a piece of Warhol. So strong was the hype around the auction that many of the collectors who would've flown in for their categories purposely stayed away. They assumed that there would be a general feeding frenzy, that the Warhol provenance would make prices skyrocket.

The unfortunate, or fortunate—it depends on how you look at it—result of such a skittish reaction was that major categories in Warhol's collection offered some bargains. His American Indian art was quite affordable simply because most of the serious collectors and dealers are from the West Coast and many of them didn't bother to show up. American Federal furniture was also reasonable, because it was assumed to be one of the most popular categories. I guess people thought: What's the point in coming to New York if they're going to get a quarter of a million for a bunch of cookie jars?

On the Sunday morning before the session when the cookie jars were to be auctioned, I received a phone call from a client of mine, who said with breathless desperation, "I need some of Andy's cookie jars."

"Well, there are a lot of them. But I have to warn you, there's a huge amount of interest in them."

"I realize that, believe me," she said.

"But if I told you afterward that you spent a thousand dollars per cookie jar, are you going to have my head?" The cookie jars had been estimated by Sotheby's to bring between $20 and $30 each (my client also knew that replicas could easily be found in a downtown shop for between $100 and $150).

"No, no; I'll give you a budget of ten thousand dollars. And try to get me ten cookie jars."

It wasn't going to be so easy.

After I got off the phone, I went downstairs to the exhibition. The cookie jars were simple ceramic cartoons in animal and human forms, which kids loved to put their fingers into. We thought so little of them that out of 175, we had illustrated only a few in the catalog. There was a group photograph of Warhol with ten jars. He had bought many of them at a Manhattan store called Pieces of Time. Each lot of cookie jars featured four or five. I made my selection based on my own taste and wrote my client's bid in my catalog.

There were 331 lots in the section of the Warhol sale in which the cookie jars fell. The bidding began at one o'clock on a Sunday afternoon, April 24, 1988. I auctioneered the first two hundred lots of what I'd call basically tchotchkes, ranging from Bakelite jewelry to beaded necklaces, unmounted faceted stones, cuff links, rings, and cigarette cases. The moment the auction rounded the bend to the toy section, I handed the gavel over to my colleague David Redden. Having a client for whom I would be bidding up to $10,000 would obviously create a conflict of interest if I were to continue as the auctioneer. At Sotheby's, this client relationship very often takes priority.

Unfortunately for my client, as soon as the first lot of cookie jars came up, two men began feverishly to duel. This lot was described as: four American pottery cookie jars comprising an American bisque yellow chick and American bisque cats, a Shawnee sailor and a rabbit in a basket, estimated at $100 to $150. David's gavel came down at $1,800. A similarly described second lot, with an identical estimate, hammered for $2,750. By the third lot they were fetching $10,500. In subsequent lots I started the bidding at $5,000 or $6,000, but the numbers quickly overshot my imposed limit. Meanwhile, the two men continued to do battle with each another. One lot went for $26,000; another went for $15,000. I realized that I was going to have a very hard time procuring any of Andy Warhol's cookie jars for my friend's kitchen.

However, as luck would have it, lot #860 was followed in the catalog by #862; a printer's error had left out #861, five cookie jars very much like the others. Before the two rabid men knew what was happening, I was able to buy the phantom lot for $5,500. My client was totally thrilled when I told her what I'd managed to do for her.

If these cookie jars were to come back on the market today, I think they'd bring a lot less, certainly nowhere near the feeding frenzy of that Sunday. They might be worth only twenty or thirty cents on those auction dollars.

Overpaying at that sale was rampant. Somehow during the heat of the sales, as his objects were brought out and spotlighted, and bidders fought tooth and nail to own something of his, the marvelous energy of Andy Warhol was brought to life again. Even I got caught up in the spirit of it all, even I grew determined to own something of his. I actually found myself bidding and overpaying $1,500 for a 999-gram block of silver, whose melt value was about $300–$400. This means that the label "Property of Andy Warhol" on this brick of pure silver cost me over $1,000. I also paid $3,000 for 100 grams of pure gold. Some time after the auction, I needed money and went to a jeweler friend of mine on Forty-seventh Street, who promptly proceeded to pull off the Andy Warhol label. "The sticker is extra weight," he informed me. "I'm not paying for that." He placed the gold on the scale and offered me what it would melt for—two thirds of what I paid—and laughed when I tried to squeeze more money out of him because the gold had once belonged to Warhol.

There was also a lot of overpaying for Warhol's Art Deco collections, primarily because of their rarity and quality. Provenance had a strong effect on the sale of an ebony oval dining table and twelve matching chairs made by Jacques-Émile Ruhlmann, circa 1926. This furniture was acquired cheaply in Paris by Warhol as, in his words, "used furniture" when he was making the film *L'Amour.* The furniture had had a lot of public exposure at the Factory, where many celebrated people had rested their elbows on the conference table/boxed-lunch tables's highly polished ebony inlay. The table, estimated at $18,000, was bid up to $72,000. The chairs, estimated at $10,000 each, sold for between $55,000 and $65,000.

The "missing jewelry" that had been found on top of Warhol's bed also received a significant amount of interest. A large gold oval Cartier wristwatch circa 1973 that was estimated at $10,000 was sold for $37,400 (I can't imagine that Warhol ever wore it); an eighteen-karat-gold, carved nephrite, colored stone, and diamond necklace by David Webb, valued at $10,000, sold for $35,200.

The last session was an evening sale of contemporary paintings. Evening sales are the only events that are ticketed. It is virtually impossible to obtain a prime seat in the main salesroom for an evening contemporary or Impressionist sale unless we virtually know your net worth and you have some history of making comparable purchases at Sotheby's. For the Warhol evening sale we had to do some judicious weeding.

The main salesroom holds a thousand people. We replaced our normal chairs, which are wide and comfortable, with a greater number of folding chairs. The walls on both sides of the salesroom were pushed away and the press lined up behind a rope on one side. There was standing room in the back of the main salesroom, but there were also two open-seating galleries equipped with television monitors—Siberia I and II—which were packed.

John Marion conducted a fierce, fast-paced bidding. A Cy Twombly that estimated at $300,000–$400,000 was bid up to $900,000 by a German dealer, the highest amount ever paid for a Twombly. A record amount of $330,000 was paid for a David Hockney drawing of, appropriately, Andy Warhol. A painting by Warhol's good friend Max Bill, inscribed "for Andy" and valued at $8,000–$12,000, was bid up to $88,000. The last breath of the Warhol sale was lot #3436, an oil painting, eighty by sixty inches, of an *Indian Cowboy with High School Jacket* by Fritz Scholder (1980). The picture was straightforward, with the figure of the Indian, somewhat older-looking than a student, dominating the canvas. It was a very American image: someone of ethnic diversity trying to fit in, trying to maintain an appearance of youth. In this way it captured something of the essence of Warhol's aesthetic. And when the hammer came down on lot #3436, at $33,000, the grand total of the contemporary art sale was $5 million.

Once the hammer fell on Warhol, John Marion announced: "Ladies and gentlemen, please take out your catalogs for our benefit auction." The Warhol evening sale was done in conjunction with an auction of fifteen paintings for AIDS, which was put together by the late Thomas Amman. This was still before the 1990s corporate vogue of giving benefits became so widespread, and I was proud that Sotheby's had donated such a prime-time slot. Any evening contemporary art sale is already, by definition, full of just the right people. We sold a Jasper Johns for $350,000, a Ross Bleckner for $80,000; and the remaining paintings brought in a total of $1,975,000.

Unexpectedly, Sotheby's did one more Warhol auction, five months later. There had been one room in Andy Warhol's town house that we never ransacked, a room upstairs of wall-to-wall filing cabinets containing Warhol's paperwork, his bills. These were his archives, and we were told they had nothing to do with the auction. After the house was emptied and the executors decided to move and reorganize these filing cabinets, in the hidden space below two bottom drawers two more bags full of jewelry were found. When they were brought to our attention, we dutifully cataloged them and announced that they would be up for sale. People kept asking why we hadn't put them in the original sale, insinuating that we had cooked up the "lost and found" scheme for our own gain. It was a little difficult to admit that we hadn't found them. And yet it was really Warhol's habit to drop his goodies wherever, in the most unexpected places, that had made this happen.

Even though there were 3,436 lots in the Warhol sale, the estate held on to many works of art, by both Warhol and his contemporaries. Shortly after the Sotheby's sale, the Warhol Estate became the Warhol Foundation, which then had to assume the value of whatever was left over from the estate, including what turned out to be seven to eight hundred boxes of detritus. Warhol had created what he called "time capsules," perhaps because, like Mrs. Rockefeller Dodge, he couldn't throw anything away—the wastebasket didn't exist in his life. No matter what he received, whether trash mail or fund-raising materials, or something left on his desk, it was automatically placed in a time capsule. His wish was that these time capsules would remain in an archive as an indication of what life was like during, for example, the week of April 26, 1972.

One of the dilemmas of any foundation or museum that inherits an estate is that often the valuable, much-sought-after objects are accompanied by vast quantities of valueless things, all of which must be preserved forever—usually as a stipulation of the bequest. The Warhol Foundation was undertaking to put on computer every single thing that was in every time capsule, an expenditure for which they were being severely criticized. Finally, they involved Sotheby's in a discussion of appraising the boxes. At one point I suggested that they do a very thorough inventory of about twenty of the boxes. I thought this would be random enough to get an idea if there might be some photographs of value, or a significant commentary by somebody of note. After this initial inventory was completed, they could come up with an average monetary estimate and then multiply.

My discussions with the foundation never got much beyond this stage. Besides the time capsules, I'd been talking to them about estimating the rest of the inventory. However, I think the foundation was rather keen on minimizing the residual value of the estate in order to try to minimize the estate tax. This is achieved by something called the "block discount."

"Block discount" means dumping a bunch of paintings by the same artist on the market at once, rendering them less valuable. In an instance such as this, it would have meant a significant difference in the tax implications. Once the foundation people realized that I was going to organize an appraisal based on fair market value, I never heard from them. Instead they went to Christie's, who used block discounts to come up with a $95 million appraisal of the rest of Warhol's estate.

If the Warhol estate was evaluated according to its probate fair market value, the Mapplethorpe was more along the lines of the estate's retail value. In fact, the Mapplethorpe executors had presented a well-thought-out plan to Christie's. Possessing between eleven thousand and twelve thousand negatives of very good pictures by Mapplethorpe, they would be able to print limited editions of these images and bring in a steady income over many years. Now, for example, if I need a good Mapplethorpe print for a charity event, I just call the Robert Miller Gallery, and they get the negative out and print one for me.

I tried to get the Mapplethorpe sale for Sotheby's. I went through the channels of my velvet mafia connections, to no avail. Despite the fact that Michael Stout, Mapplethorpe's lawyer and executor, is a very good friend of mine, the sale went to Christie's. I believe that this was the result of Sotheby's tenuous relationship with Sam Wagstaff, Mapplethorpe's late lover. Wagstaff was a great collector of photography and nineteenth-century American silver. Before his death—which preceded Mapplethorpe's—Wagstaff contacted our appraisal department about valuing his collection. Unfortunately, we sent a generalist from the Arcade, the department that handles our less-valuable items, and when he looked at Wagstaff's, shall we say, eclectic collection of American Victorian silver, to determine the estimate he just weighed everything and multiplied the weight by $4 an ounce. Though I can understand why Mr. Wagstaff might have been put off by such a calculation, that is the only true way to arrive at an estimate. On the basis of the estimate, people decide how much they want to pay.

Wagstaff determined that his things would be sold anywhere *but* Sotheby's; and it seems those wounded feelings carried through to when Mapplethorpe's executors were deciding what to do with his estate. Christie's auctioned Mapplethorpe in 1989. Ironically, in 1994, Stout asked me to sell a very late small painting by Vuillard, which had gone unsold in the original sale. Christie's had placed what I call a Japanese estimate on it: $200,000–$300,000; but no Japanese conglomerates had come after it. I kidded Stout about the irony of the

situation, but then told him quite frankly that Christie's estimate was ridiculously high. He didn't want to deal with
Christie's anymore. The picture was sent over, and we placed
an estimate of $40,000–$60,000 on it; and it brought $70,000,
which is really what it's worth. It seems fitting that I sold the
last gasp of the Mapplethorpe estate. What goes around comes
around.

14. Charity Auctions

Many years ago, I used to go down to the Monmouth racetrack in New Jersey and do an auction for the Monmouth County Mental Health Association. I would sell miscellaneous items, little bits of jewelry, a gift certificate. The grand prize would always be a trip to somewhere nice. The event was chaired by the wife of Leon Hess, of Hess Oil, who owned half the racetrack. I remember feeling panicked when I did the first of these events. Unlike the auctions at Sotheby's, which were attended by people who had come specifically to bid on one thing or another, a racetrack auction was a wild card, and sometimes lots came up that no one bid on. Fortunately, Leon Hess always sat in the front row, chomping on a cigar. And if the bidding slackened, I'd start to stare at him mercilessly, and up would pop his hand. He knew what he had to do—otherwise he'd have to go home later and deal with an unhappy spouse.

The first time I was approached by Gay Men's Health Crisis was in 1982, when they asked me to donate money to buy a block of tickets to Ringling Bros. Circus, their first fundraiser. By 1983, GMHC had gotten a little more ambitious and came to me with the idea of having a benefit art auction. I went to the president of Sotheby's, Jim Lally, and to John Marion, who was at that time chairman of Sotheby's North America. The company was in the middle of the hostile takeover attempt by Stephen Swid and Marshall Cogan; and '82–'83 was that terrible year in the art business. It was suggested to me that I align myself with someone such as Mathilde Krim and the AIDS Medical Foundation before approaching Sotheby's.

I was shocked to be deterred. And I was embarrassed corporately, in the sense that I was not able to get Sotheby's to agree to do the auction. I'm sorry to say that the reason I was unable to get their support was all in the word "gay." Or, more specifically, "Gay Men's Health Crisis." If the name had been Manhattan Health Crisis, I believe that auction would've happened at Sotheby's. Basically I had been told to affiliate my efforts with Mathilde Krim because her cause was perceived as being somewhat more "straight."

And so the first art auction for GMHC took place at Phillips, a smaller auction house, also based in Britain. I wasn't the auctioneer, but I was very involved in the event. I donated a lot of time and a lot of inventory, and I also bought a lot of things. Sotheby's soon got over its initial trepidation about working with GMHC. As it turned out, the late president of the board of GMHC, Nathan Kolodner, worked at the André Emmerich Gallery. Once John Marion realized that Nathan was involved and that local dealers were dedicating their time, he wanted to be part of it. Each subsequent GMHC auction has taken place at Sotheby's. AIDS causes have become stronger by overcoming preconceptions and resistance, one CEO at a time.

Those early benefit auctions transpired in a very straight-forward style, not much different from their prototypes: estate auctions and evening sales of painting and European art and Americana. There was no banter with the audience, no egging on the bidders or identifying them by name. But then, after the unprecedented sale of the birdhouses in Southampton and after Jeffrey's death, I found my voice as an auctioneer in front of a lot of very prominent and socially conscious Manhattanites. And as they watched me develop my new style, they inundated me with requests to auctioneer their own benefits.

Suddenly I was in great demand as an auctioneer. I also found myself more in demand socially. Prominent, wealthy women who patronized charities religiously and supported arts causes devoutly—and had husbands who would often rather stay at home—thought I made a great date. There's an old cliché that it takes twenty years to become an overnight success.

And so besides becoming a celebrated auctioneer, I became what's known in the business as a "walker," a professional extra man. A lot of people like to look down on this avocation, but I'd like to state for the record that being a professional extra man is a very important job in New York—especially if the woman who needs such a man is going to be contributing her time and her money to one of the man's fund-raisers or benefits. Thus, just as I make it easy for people to spend their money when I'm up on the auction block, I can donate my services on a Monday, Tuesday, or Thursday night to a woman in a beautiful dress who wears the best jewelry. Quite often, the husband of this woman, whoever he might be, is so glad to stay home and watch the football game that he doesn't put up too much of a fuss if she donates a nice charitable chunk to a tax-deductible cause. I don't mind admitting that there are a number of us, mostly gay, who help the husbands of these women out. We're not a threat, we're fun to be with, and there are no strings attached.

⟨⟨⨀ ⨀⟩⟩

Shortly after Jeffrey died, Mrs. Lawrence Copley Thaw, a good friend of mine, called up and said that there was an organization called Save Venice. Many Americans were donating $1,000 to this fund, which got them four complete days of lectures and tours of palazzi that were never open to the public. At the end of the four days, a black-tie ball would be given for five hundred people. The $1,000 did not include the price of one's travel or hotel. "You need to get away, Robert," she said. "I'm on the board of the event. I'm inviting you, and you don't have to pay." I said, "I'd love to do this, but I don't want to be kept." I sent my $1,000.

Now, a couple of walker friends of mine, who shall remain anonymous, said that was a silly thing to do. And I have since learned that the Walker Handbook of Etiquette disagrees with me and is predicated on freebies. But my method of being a walker is Dutch all the way. Even if the husband has already paid for the tickets, I still like to cover my share. "Madam, you buy yours and I'll buy mine"—I think that's a much more elegant way to move through life. "I can't afford you and I don't want to be kept."

As it turned out, a lot of people who took that trip to Venice had known Jeffrey and knew me. They all were extremely solicitous and kind. And my, let's call it, nascent renown eradicated any awkward speculation such as "So who is *she* shacked up with?" In 1987, I was forty-three, too old to be taken for somebody's son, the perfect age to be embarking on a new social career. The word got out that I was loose, I was free, I was available, and then the phone started to ring.

I also became a professional guest, a social phenomenon that I have refined to a near art form. In fact, my only real competition in the professional guest arena has been Fran Lebowitz, who once said that professional guests provide a great service to people with large homes, because it's our job to help them enjoy their manses. It's our duty, as a matter of fact. I basically have four rules about guesting—that is, provided I'm allowed to bring my two dogs. It's my only requirement; otherwise I'm a dream on wheels.

My first rule is to take a pushy house present. If one asks what constitutes pushy, I say in the hundreds. Or something antique that I might know about but my hosts might not and will be flattered by.

Rule number two is to provide at least one major meal. I either cook it myself or take everyone out. This is where I think I might leave Ms. Lebowitz in the dust. But then, she makes it up in witty repartee and a state-of-the-art sense of humor.

Rule number three is to overtip if there is staff. This translates to around $15 for one person, $25 for a couple, per day.

Rule number four is I make my own bed.

I've never had a desire to own a house, because I have lots of friends who have very nice ones on which they've spent fortunes. I just don't have an edifice complex. Everybody I know has a house in the country, and I basically know where they all are for the rest of their lives of weekends. I don't want to be so predictable.

I make up my schedule for the summer in March. I start calling the people whom I really want to visit and book up my prime weekends with them. I give a choice of several weekends; this way nobody feels hemmed in or obligated. And if I've overtipped their staff in previous years, the staff is always happy to see me. "Oh, Mr. Woolley is coming out for the weekend" causes them visibly to brighten.

As the late eighties ended and the nineties began, I found myself getting more and more involved in all kinds of benefit causes. The first true fantasy auction I ever did was for Marianne Williamson's Center for Living in Los Angeles. By 1990, I had refined my maverick auctioneering style, and my reputation had preceded me. The event was held in an airplane hangar in Santa Monica, and a lot of wonderful one-of-a-kind things were offered. There was a crowd of about three thousand people.

When Marianne Williamson first contacted me, I encouraged her to conjure up fantasy-type inventories. "It can't be just fashion dresses and contemporary paintings, antiques, and conventional vacation trips," I said. After all, Williamson has the support of powerful people within the Hollywood community; the whole benefit, in fact, was underwritten by Hollywood. She could pick up the phone and tell Dolly Parton that we'd love to auction a special visit to Dollywood, Tennessee, that would include dinner with Ms. Parton. She could ask Lauren Bacall if we could auction her services to record the message on an answering machine. For a charity auction to do extremely well, you must offer things that you cannot buy for money, any amount of money, at any other time. Even if you're doing a benefit auction in Detroit, there's got to be some local celebrity—a mayor, an actor who made it in Hollywood, a sports star—who has a mystique and is renowned for having a beautiful home, a good golf game, or some such thing, which can be easily packaged, promoted, and sold.

The Los Angeles event was studded with celebrities. I had Elizabeth Taylor sitting in the front row and batting her violet eyes at me, Barry Diller sitting next to Anjelica Huston, David Geffen sitting next to Cher. Before I went on, there was an incredible fashion show, in which all the dresses that were modeled were tag-sold.

When I stepped up onto the stage, I said, "Will the ladies and gentlemen who are running the lights please take those spots off me. I have a very big ego, don't question that for a minute, but I need to *see* the money, and those things blind me, so please shut them off."

The first fantasy lot I auctioned was for thirty-two children and four adult chaperones to meet Michael Jackson at his ranch for a picnic and a screening (this, I reiterate, was in 1990, which I feel I must interject as a point of reference and not as any humorous commentary). When I opened up the bidding at $500, three thousand hands went up. Obviously, I had started too low, so I jumped to $5,000, and there still seemed to be thousands of hands. The waving began thinning out only after I passed $10,000, but the bidding trotted all the way up to $55,000.

As it turned out, the underbidder was so upset not to have won that I got a very clever idea. Sandy Gallin, one of the more powerful managers in Hollywood, who was in charge of Michael Jackson's life in many regards, had a word with the rock star. Jackson generously agreed to offer the same afternoon again, on another day, for the same price. So that particular fantasy lot was worth $110,000.

The other great favor I sold was offered by one of the cochairs of the event, the artist David Hockney. He had volunteered to paint the inside of a swimming pool. I knew that this would be a lively lot. Not only is Hockney among the most prominent painters of the late twentieth century—his work on canvas is worth hundreds of thousands of dollars—but much of his work has been about people diving into, dangling their legs in, or lying beside pools. And I knew that Californians had very keen affections for their pools.

As it happened, Lester Perskey, a Hollywood producer I've known for twenty years, arrived at the event with a cheap ticket, which meant he was seated beyond the rope, on the periphery. I saw him moaning about it, and I quite generously told him that he could take my very cushy seat up front, next to his friend Francine LeFrak, while I was working. So he was sitting right below me during the auction.

When "Hockney will paint your swimming pool" came up, Lester started bidding on it, as did many other people, at $10,000. But when the price reached $50,000, Lester dropped out. And that's when I said, "Lester Perskey, you are a very rich and very successful producer. How dare you stop bidding?"

"Oh, all right," he said, and plunged back into the bidding again. $65,000, $70,000, $80,000. Finally, it was just Lester against a man on my left. And as the price kept rising, the three thousand people in the audience went crazy. It was a joy to embarrass Lester into bidding. I didn't worry about it, because I knew he could easily afford this little folly. He won at $110,000. "Now I've got to build a swimming pool so he can paint on it," Perskey joked as he had his photograph taken with Hockney.

Although people seemed to think it was wonderfully extravagant for Lester to pay David Hockney $110,000 to paint a real estate fixture, something that was immovable, I think

Perskey made out like a bandit. There are probably only two swimming pools in the world that Hockney has painted, and Lester's is one of them. Hockney did a few smaller preparatory drawings as well as a mural-size study of the swimming pool, which Lester hung on his walls. So in the end he got some drawings, a mural, and a painted swimming pool for $110,000.

Friends in Deed, a charity founded by Mike Nichols and Cynthia O'Neil, is an affiliate of Marianne Williamson's Manhattan Center for Living. Once, in the late eighties, Nichols allowed me to auction a walk-on part in his film *Regarding Henry,* starring Harrison Ford. It went for $40,000 to a member of the Rockefeller family, Mary Gilbert. She got to play a political dignitary's wife, who says something along the lines of "I had such fun at your party. It was wonderful. Good night." The underbidder was Bobby Taubman (the son of Al Taubman, the chairman of Sotheby's), who was trying to buy it for his very attractive wife, Linda. It had been a horse race between these two bidders, with Bobby on the phone with Linda. At $40,000 he thought he saw the warning light and dropped out. I'd told him ahead of time that all of it was tax deductible except for the standard fee for a walk-on part, which was $250.

The next day, he called me and said that his wife was very upset not to have won, and he wanted to surprise her. Could I possibly call up Mike Nichols and offer him $40,000 for another walk-on part, the proceeds of which would similarly go to Friends in Deed? I did what I was asked to do, and Nichols was understanding but explained that with all the editing that goes on in a film, it's difficult enough to keep one walk-on part in the final product. Two would be nearly impossible; it would unnecessarily compromise his integrity. He was forced to decline.

During the late eighties, The Gap began a series of advertisements, which appeared in magazines and on bus shelters, of mostly but not always young up-and-coming artists, designers, actors, singers, painters, and writers wearing Gap T-shirts and jeans. These photo ads were by famous photographers and described who the subjects were, as well as listing their accomplishments. Very much admired and talked about, the advertisements created instant publicity and a hint of cachet. In the best of them, the subjects weren't too obviously famous; when you looked at them, you were made to feel that the people wearing jeans came from all walks of life.

I believe that the man who bid $55,000 for the privilege of being photographed for a series of six-page ads would've paid practically anything to be in them. Anything. When you find something that will inspire this kind of feeding frenzy, you've struck gold in the fantasy auction arena.

In April 1994, I did an auction for the Rainforest Foundation, the favorite charity of the singer Sting. Sting's wife, Trudi Styler, produces this benefit concert every year at Carnegie Hall, and '94 featured an extraordinary lineup of artistic talent, including Luciano Pavarotti, Tammy Wynette, Whitney Houston, Wynton Marsalis, Elton John, and Rod Stewart, among others. It was a magical musical evening. After the concert, at around 11:00 P.M., twelve hundred people went to the Waldorf-Astoria for dinner. Between the main course and dessert, there were between six and eight lots to sell. Elton John had been asked to be the auctioneer. But he had said, "No, no, that would be a mistake; you must get my friend Robert Woolley," and the auctioneering was delegated to me.

This was the quintessential big-time deluxe fantasy auction. Not only did it attract interesting objects; it was heavily attended by luminaries in New York society, entertainment celebrities, as well as prominent businessmen. A good portion of the event had been underwritten by Ron Perlman and Revlon. Perlman captured the spirit of the auction by bidding impulsively for a four-wheel-drive Land Rover that, though fully loaded, was not new. The car had been on safari in Costa Rica and was worth retail around $38,000. When the bidding reached $39,000, I announced to the audience, "We are now in tax-deductible land."

"Tax-deductible land" sounded like the magical place where everyone wanted to be—this kind of fancy-free spending of money for something gossamer and one-of-a-kind was in itself part of the thrill of it all. Perlman, who was sitting at Sting's table, bought the Land Rover for $69,000. Blaine and Robert Trump donated four tickets worth $50–$75 apiece to a New York Knicks playoff game, which Anna Wintour, the editor of *Vogue*, won for $10,000. Gianni Versace, who was one of the event's benefactors, donated a couture dress, which Sting bought for his wife.

Traditionally, anyone who spends thousands of dollars on pieces of clothing will never do it off somebody else's body. Bill Blass has very generously given $3,000 gift certificates for his line of clothing—for this sort of divertissement I can usually get a little more than $3,000. But selling an actual dress in size eight off someone's back is usually a "no thank you very much." Only once did I jump into such a situation, and that was a very special occasion.

Working an AIDS benefit in Atlanta in 1991, I had arrived late, without much of a chance to look at what was being offered. I was auctioneering in the middle of a hotel ballroom with about four hundred people. Dinner had been served. An attractive young man came out wearing lot #4, a Versace couture tuxedo donated by Elton John. It was bright red, fire en-

gine red, nothing subtle about it; it was red, red, red. On occasion I have been known to see something I like on offer and
bid for it. Usually I try to make arrangements beforehand with
somebody in the audience, who will bid for me. In Atlanta, I
was wearing my usual black tux, and on a whim, I said aloud,
"That looks like it might fit me." So with four hundred people watching me disrobe, I took off my black tuxedo and put
on the Elton/Versace one. Apart from the length of the sleeves,
it basically fit like a glove. So I proceeded to bid on it myself,
with competition from the room. I was public about it, telling
the audience I could use it at events like that one. "I'm delighted that Elton was so generous as to give away this costume."

Once the bidding reached $900, however, nobody would
go any higher. I said to the audience, "I'm getting a bargain
here," but it didn't make a difference. After all, how many people can get away with wearing a red tuxedo? I won.

When I was introduced to Elton John a few months later,
I said, "You know, I bought your red tuxedo, the one you gave
to the AIDS Atlanta Auction," and he was amused. He asked
what I'd paid for it, and when I answered around $1,000, he
looked at me and said with a big smile, "I think we paid
Versace ten thousand dollars for that thing." Now I was truly
delighted to have the Elton John tuxedo, glad I wasn't the
one to buy it retail from Gianni Versace. This was a circumstance where it was not the *provenance,* Elton John, but the
color that kept it from bringing more money. I wear that red
tuxedo quite a lot. If it's recycled after my life, perhaps the combination of Elton John and Robert Woolley will bring a fairer
price.

15. How To

I believe that Americans are generous people. New Yorkers—well, many of them—go over the top. I would guess that in Manhattan alone, with the hundreds of benefits that take place every year, hundreds of millions of dollars are raised. Often, between the two peak seasons—early October to early December and then April to early June—there are several significant events on the same evening. Both *Town & Country* and *Avenue* list the major events months in advance, so that patrons can keep their calendars straight.

West of the Hudson River, benefit events almost always take place on a Saturday night, but in New York City, weekends are considered unsuitable. People leave for the weekends and are unavailable. And because the people with the most money to give often claim they have the most stressful of lives, it is inconsiderate to interrupt their weekends in the country or at the beach.

I've been very involved in giving benefits for nearly ten years. I have observed a lot of successful evenings, and I've watched some unmitigated disasters. It's hard to get it right on the first try, and through paying attention and lots of trial and error, I've made a few observations and learned a few tricks about putting on a benefit.

There are two reasons for attending a benefit. Either you believe in the cause or your arm is being twisted socially. And I believe, perhaps cynically, that it's usually the latter. Because of this, the evening must cater especially to those who might easily get bored and who might otherwise feel as though they've been roped into something.

My first rule is that it's not really worth putting on a benefit in New York unless you know it can raise six figures, hopefully more. I know this sounds presumptuous, but I have found that the only kind of affair that can generate interest year after year is a great one, and great ones require a substantial investment in catering, a band, and a suitable venue. To justify these kinds of expenses, to make the undertaking worthwhile, you need to realize a very substantial profit.

My second rule is to ensure that the event lets out at a reasonable hour. Ten-thirty P.M. is my suggestion. Aim to begin the event at seven, with cocktails served away from the dining area. This translates to seven-thirty, because benefits invariably run twenty to thirty minutes late. If you want to repeat the event year after year, your patrons—the husbands in particular, who have to get up early the next morning—should remember that it wasn't too late a night. And when people are talking about it the next day, as they always do, you don't want them to be tired and cranky.

To make this happen, you want to keep the event bureaucratically streamlined. When too many people are involved in a benefit—and want to take credit for it or be at least visually acknowledged—they feel compelled to get up and make long-winded speeches thanking everyone involved and banging on and on about the cause. They don't quite realize that most people have already paid their money and now just want to have fun; they certainly don't need to have the cause jammed down their throats. Patrons cannot be expected to have the same emotional investment as the people running a benefit. Therefore, any spoken address should be kept to a bare minimum.

Every year I do the live auction for the National Center for Learning Disabilities, which is chaired by Anne Ford, one of society's grandes dames, a compassionate woman who is dedicated to this charity. After collaborating with Anne for several years, I hazarded to speak to her about the way she was running the event. I mentioned minimizing the speeches, and then I said, "And for God's sake, don't show a video."

She looked at me timidly and said, "But it's only seven minutes long."

"Don't you remember what happened last year?" I asked. "Two minutes into the video, everybody started talking to one another."

"Okay, okay, you're right. I'll cut it down to two minutes next time," she conceded, which she did at the 1995 benefit.

In my opinion, one should never take the Jerry Lewis approach. Don't get me wrong, he's been a major force in fundraising, and I would never knock him, but for the sake of good taste, I feel that it's inappropriate to trot out a "challenged" individual while the audience is eating their salmon mousse in the Grand Ballroom of the Plaza Hotel. That is not the moment or the method to pull on the heartstrings.

In terms of apparel, I strongly suggest black-tie formal, because it gives women the opportunity to buy a new dress, to have their hair done perfectly, to show off. Fortunately, a benefit gala is one of the few remaining circumstances where one can dress in this manner and not look foolish. In society at the turn of the century, formal meant white tie and informal meant black tie. Men wore white tie, a cape, a stovepipe hat, and carried a cane to the opera; women wore tiaras. For a private dinner party, men dressed in black tie. Today formal means black tie, and informal means dark business suit. Many people wear blue jeans and a T-shirt to the opera, and the only white-tie event left is the New York Philharmonic benefit, and everybody, especially the men, complains about it.

If there are awards to be given, keep the presentation short and sweet. The worst kind of benefit I've ever seen is the sort that gives, say, a glass apple to a CEO in a hotel where you dine on rubbery chicken. There are more of these events than anything else; they tend to be very corporate and therefore very tedious. My advice is: just get on with it. "Ladies and gentlemen, can I have your attention, please. Nancy Kissinger." Once when I was MC'ing a benefit for Casita Maria, a Hispanic settlement house that has been around for decades, I was asked to introduce Ralph Lauren, who was presenting Casita Maria's gold medal to Audrey Hepburn. The day of the event, the Lauren people faxed me fifteen single-spaced pages on who he was and what he'd done. I took the fax with me when I got up on the stage. Showing it to the audience, I said, "I received this today. Ralph Lauren's office sent it to me, in case I'd forgotten anything about him. This condenses down to 'Ladies and gentlemen, Ralph Lauren.' "

Getting celebrities such as Lauren involved is obviously key to putting on a good benefit. To secure celebrities, you often have to do some heavy-duty social arm-twisting. You need a celebrity's name at the top of the invitation to get people's attention, because these days there's enormous competition for charitable dollars in this town. Never ask to use the name of somebody famous if he or she is not planning to show up. The patrons will take note that the celebrity was not delivered and they may not attend the following year.

I have developed a sixth sense about benefits. When I get a printed invitation, I can read who is at the top of the page and who is the vice chair, and know if these celebs are actually going to show. If you're hosting a new benefit, try to target a celebrity who will be reliable and will have drawing power. Youngish people, particularly actors, might be appropriate for juvenile causes, but they're generally unreliable and it is probably wise to avoid them. Obviously, in the beginning, most any celebrity will have to do, but once the benefit gets established, be as judicious as possible.

One person who has been very generous with her time is Joan Rivers. Joan and I met the year that Jeffrey and her husband died. The first time we met, we discussed their lives and their deaths and formed a special bond. Joan is the sort of person who can hardly say no if somebody calls her with a good cause. I'm in the habit of auctioning dinner for thirty people at my house, with Joan Rivers as the guest of honor. Whoever wins the bid arranges it with Joan's schedule and invites thirty people to come have dinner with her at my place.

I can think of only one person these days who might lend her name to the top of the page and get away with not showing: Hillary Rodham Clinton. Everybody knows that her coming would be a miracle and more hassle than it's worth, because of the Secret Service escorts.

Salman Rushdie is another one, but that goes without saying.

Seating for dinner should happen by eight-thirty, nine at

the latest. And wine should *not* be served at table until after the first course. You don't want to get people too tipsy too soon.

The first course should be something neutral and good-looking enough to be waiting on the table: smoked trout, smoked salmon, not something like salad, which can look wilted if it's put out forty-five minutes before the guests arrive. In lieu of using hotel staff, I personally prefer a good caterer, such as Glorious Food, a Manhattan company whose staff are great-looking; Glorious Food is used by most of the A-list benefits. A good caterer assigns more waiters per table and can handle the transition of plates without causing a racket. Don't expect to book a hotel and bring your own caterer, however; unfortunately it doesn't work that way. If you go the hotel route, you are obligated to use their union staff.

The main course should be adventuresome. Veal has been terribly overused. My current favorite entrée is chicken pot pie. The golden crust looks appetizing; everything you want to eat is right in the pie. Dessert could be sorbet done in three colors, or ice cream. Cookies to nibble on are always nice.

Let's dance. It's critical to hire a band that plays good, hip music that will inspire dancing. The band should be playing when the guests are first milling into the dining area. And the band should play all through the meal and afterward. The leader should be informed ahead of time when to tone down the volume of the music during the food courses.

A live auction isn't mandatory, but it does perk up the evening. Timing is key. It should take place between the entrée and dessert; twelve lots is a good number. You're subliminally telling the patrons, "You don't get dessert until you spend more of your money." And the live auction should ideally be of the fantasy kind; you're selling the best things that are the hardest to find: a ski week at the house of a celebrity in Sun Valley; a diving lesson by Greg Louganis. Such whimsies require a lot of work on the part of the benefit's organizers: at least twenty phone calls per lot and importuning the CEO of an airline company to donate a round-trip ticket to Tahiti. To sell the frivolous things like trips and cruises, have a good lightfooted, charismatic auctioneer. And once you've mastered Robert Woolley's Benefit Rules, then you can break them.

◖◗

The fact that Jeffrey Childs and I had a "white marriage" for the last seven years of his life was not generally known among the masses of people, including the entire staff of Sotheby's, who attended his funeral. All throughout that beautifully orchestrated occasion at Saint Thomas More Church on East Eighty-ninth Street, people kept coming up to me and asking me how I was. "I'm fine," I kept telling them. "I'm HIV-negative. I'm fine." And believe me, I was determined to stay that way. I knew firsthand what death from AIDS was like. I had lived as close to the edge of that kind of dying as was humanly possible. I was forty-three years old, with presumably a long life ahead of me.

But in 1988 I fell in love with the priapic Michael Meehan and went from having sex perhaps two or three times a year to having sex two or three times a day. Michael, a gifted decorative painter, was, to put it mildly, highly charged. And during the first few years I was with him, we used the most expensive condoms one could buy, skin-sensitive and made of lambskin—which, I later learned from my doctor, prevent pregnancy but are too porous to prevent the transmission of the AIDS virus.

Because we were both operating under the assumption that we were having safe sex, Michael withheld the truth of his own status from me until he began to get symptoms. In early 1989, he developed a lump on the back of his neck that turned out to be a lesion of Kaposi's sarcoma, a purplish skin cancer that many doctors now feel is aggravated by the use of amyl nitrites, or "poppers." I never had any suspicions about my health until the summer of 1989, when Michael and I were traveling in Italy and I came down with a fever in Ravello, a fever that lasted two weeks and only abated when we finally reached Venice. One of the earliest symptoms of AIDS can be a flulike illness that occurs within a very short time of being infected.

A bit concerned about my health, in September 1989 I went for another AIDS test. When I returned to my doctor's office to be given the grim news that I was now HIV-positive, I can't say that I was shocked. I received the truth of my new status with a fatalistic attitude, knowing I had only my ignorance to blame for the state of my health. And though I was angry at the twist of fate, I was determined to make sure everyone I knew would not make the same mistake I had.

I got my first T-cell count several months after my positive test results, when I became involved in a vaccine trial in Boston Deaconess Hospital with Dr. Jerome Groopman. My T cells were at 500, just below the normal range of 600 to 1,200, and that qualified me for the trial. No one knew if the vaccine would be any good, and one of the doctors explained that injecting me with bio-engineered GP 120 might end up being like prescribing chicken soup for a broken leg. It might not help a great deal, but it certainly wouldn't hurt.

For two years I ran up to Boston for my injections. In those days I was full of hope. I was in the early stages, I was still healthy, still able to deny that the end might be coming. AIDS activism was on the rise, more money was being spent by the government; surely there'd be some kind of breakthrough that would at the very least be able to prolong my life. But it turned out that the vaccine never worked in any serious way. And I suppose that initial trial and error became the blueprint for the rest of my relationship with AIDS.

Although my T cells continued to decline over the next few years, I still felt pretty well. I got more involved in charity work, particularly events that benefited AIDS. As I sensed a shade of something moving inevitably toward me, I became more outrageous and flamboyant in my auctioneering antics, even more outspoken as an activist. There was little that I wouldn't do or say if it helped a good cause.

The autumn of 1993 marked a culmination for me. I celebrated my twenty-fifth aniversary working at Sotheby's and was only a few months away from my fiftieth birthday, on January 1, 1994. And on a more personal note I realized that I would probably face the end of my life surrounded by close friends, the families of people I have formed around me, but without an intimate relationship.

Michael Meehan and I had broken up in 1992 and he was already in a new relationship. Despite the rupture, we had managed to remain in close contact; I accepted his new relationship, and his new lover became my friend. This may sound incestuous, or perhaps foolishly magnanimous, but when you know your time is limited, when your death is looming, the ego has a tendency to shrink. Trying to survive has a way of banishing frivolity and making certain things black and white, especially when you and the people surrounding you are fighting against the same foe.

On a whim I decided to turn my yearly Halloween party into a paid event to benefit Gay Men's Health Crisis, of which I'm a board member. I got Sotheby's to agree to host the event in the main salesroom of the auction house. With the help of Michael and a few of my staff members, I sent out invitations to 2,800 friends and clients. In a break from the tradition of previous years, people would have to pay to attend my Halloween/birthday party: old friends were expected to pay $500; new friends, $250; and acquaintances, $125. And they would not be admitted unless they came in some kind of costume. Halloween fell on a Sunday.

When I first discussed the event with Dede, she asked me point-blank how many people would be in drag.

"That's the most homophobic thing you've ever asked," I told her. "How can I possibly know? It's not Woolley's drag ball."

"I just want to know what to expect."

"I can't predict what people will wear. I'm sure a lot of people will come in drag. It's going to be quite exotic."

October is traditionally a busy month for Sotheby's in terms of auctions. In fact, an Impressionist painting sale was slated to be held a few days after my party. At five o'clock on Sunday afternoon, the salesroom was full of people looking at the million-dollar daubs of the Impressionists. Moments later the gallery closed, the paintings that had contributed to revolutionizing the art market were recessed, and decorators from Castle & Pierpont began (pro bono) festooning the salesroom with cornstalks and pumpkins and, to the horror of Dede

Brooks, one hundred bales of hay that I had ordered without her knowledge. The hay was a fire hazard and, I suspect, was probably illegal. In my exuberance to make a great event, I'd forgotten about the fact that people would be smoking.

Out of a thousand guests, six hundred came to the party in serious drag costumes. Few were in formal attire; those who were wore masks.

I was dressed in an Elizabethan costume with a white-ruffed neck. Michael Meehan and his new lover, Sebastian, arrived early, clad scantily, like a pair of pornographic court jesters, in codpieces. They stood with me at the top of the stairs while I greeted people. When Dede Brooks arrived dressed as a Matisse and took in the sight of two nearly naked men next to me, she said somewhat admonishingly, "I thought this was going to be in good taste."

"A costume party in good taste?" I said. "Believe me, you haven't seen anything yet."

Somewhat overwhelmed, Dede disappeared into the party and after forty-five minutes realized that what Michael and Sebastian were wearing was hardly daring in comparison with the more elaborate and often more scandalous outfits, including drag numbers, that were worn by some very prominent people, among them clients who had, in more sober moments, spent millions of dollars on art in this very salesroom. Male business tycoons arrived dressed as divas, one of the most prominent realtors in New York, Robby Brown, came as Ivana Trump, female corporate heads regaled themselves in dominatrix leather. When the receipts of my Halloween benefit were finally tallied, I had raised $240,000 for GMHC.

16. The Curse

The irony of my life now is that practically everybody says, "You've never looked better." What they mean is that I've finally slimmed down to fighting weight.

"Well, I'm on the wrong diet," I say, wishing I felt as good as everybody says I look.

"You have a lot of color in your face," they say. "Have you been to the beach?"

"Beach color, the latest tint by Bactrim," I'll say. Bactrim is one of the medications I take, a prophylactic against PCP pneumonia, and it causes ruddiness. "Fortunately, it hasn't turned me blue."

This may sound flippant, but it is a typical conversation I have had with people who ask me how I am feeling but don't really want to know. They want me to tell them that I'm fine because they have trouble dealing with the fact that I might be dying. Alas, I tell them what they want to hear. Only if a friend asks me do I literally delve into how I am.

A few months after the Halloween benefit, during the winter of 1994, my health began suddenly to unravel. I came down with the same candidiasis, or "oral thrush," that Jeffrey had

had. I lost thirty pounds from a sudden deadening of appetite—truly disconcerting for someone who normally loves to eat—and my T cells dropped below 200, which is one of the clinical definitions of AIDS. When I was diagnosed, I had a choice: minimize my condition to others until it was absolutely necessary to succumb to the illness, or tell people about it while I was still relatively healthy, go public and be an example of somebody living with AIDS.

Throughout last winter and spring, there were persistent rumors at work about my health, and at one point Dede Brooks approached me to say that she was having Mary Fisher come to Sotheby's to speak at the monthly staff meeting that all employees are asked to attend. Mary Fisher, who made such a stunning speech about being HIV-positive at the 1992 Republican National Convention, is the stepdaughter of our vice chairman Max Fisher. When Dede asked if I would introduce Mary, I think this was her delicate way of suggesting that I might use the opportunity to speak about myself. There was too much hubbub going on about my condition. Everyone knows me as the upbeat, paternal force who keeps peace in the land. Maintaining that facade had become more and more difficult. During the spring of 1994, I was generally perceived as being depressed much of the time, which was greatly at odds with my reputation for being full of life. Now, I knew I might depress other people by what I had to say, but I also knew that clinical depression can be one of the symptoms of AIDS.

Telling Dede that I'd be happy to introduce Mary Fisher, I made a mental note that perhaps it would be an appropriate opportunity to tell the entire Sotheby's staff that I had AIDS. The idea of making such a public announcement was unnerving, but I realized I had to do it.

In the weeks before Mary Fisher's scheduled appearance, I made a point of taking aside each of the twenty department heads and telling them that I had AIDS. Judging by how I'd seen and heard news travel in the past, I assumed that once I'd told these people, the word of my illness would spread all over the company. By the time I made my public announcement, everyone would already know. But this turned out not to be the case.

Around two weeks before Mary Fisher's scheduled appearance, Michael Meehan died. His death was another great blow to me, and the people in my life claim never to have seen me so despondent. In the midst of my sadness over his death, I had trouble envisioning myself standing before the entire company and telling them my news.

And so I was in a terrible and very uncharacteristic state of nerves on Monday, June 13, 1994, when I arrived at Sotheby's at five o'clock in the afternoon. I felt that I just couldn't face the staff meeting that would soon take place. Mary Fisher had already arrived and was sitting in Dede Brooks's office. I was brought in to be introduced to her, and when Dede mentioned my introduction I became very shrill and said, "I don't know if I can do anything like this today."

Dede smartly concluded the meeting, and once Mary Fisher was brought downstairs, she walked briskly across the room and grabbed both of my arms. "Robert," she said with tears in her eyes, "you've got to get hold of yourself. You don't have to do anything you don't want to do. But I can't bear to see you like this. Nor can anybody else. We all love you. We want to help you. But you have to let us."

"I feel so terrible," I said. "I feel so incredibly low."

"I know," she said. "I understand. So, how about if I introduce Mary."

Thinking that I would be telling the staff of Sotheby's I had AIDS, my two dearest friends, Judy Peabody and David Jackson, had come to sit with me. Dede introduced Mary Fisher, who spoke for around twenty minutes about living with the virus, about fighting against the stigma and the prejudices, about being a mother and telling her children about her illness. Everyone, and especially I, was moved by her bravery. And as her talk went on, I felt something beginning to lift. I soon grew aware of my own compulsion to speak. Once Mary's talk was completed, she received a standing ovation.

How she knew I was ready, I'll never quite understand. Perhaps it was a mutual recognition between two waning souls. And yet in the midst of her applause, Mary Fisher came over to give me a hug and very gently led me toward the microphone. It was the first time in my life that standing at a podium felt somewhat unnatural. As I looked out over the gathering of familiar faces, it was as if all those years of auctioneering fell away, as if billions of dollars of art had never been sold under my gavel and I were beginning all over again. What suddenly lay before me was a territory as new as auctioning lost-and-found articles had been when I was a sophomore at Drew University.

"I'm at a loss for words," I said to the hushed room. And then I said, "But you know that's really not true." And that got a laugh. I proceeded to tell the staff of Sotheby's that I had used the wrong type of condom and that the least I could do was tell people that if they used a lambskin condom, the more expensive kind, they might prevent pregnancy, but that was it. They may be more expensive and sensual, but they are not protective. Use latex. If somebody as sophisticated as I had made such a dumb mistake, then others could too. "I'm not pregnant," I said to the staff of Sotheby's. "But I have AIDS."

A shiver went through the room, and that surprised me. I learned later that all the department heads had kept my news to themselves. They treated it like a secret. I respected them for that, but this was the sort of thing that I now had to dispel. A public figure going public with AIDS is one of the most powerful ways that this disease and its stigmas can be fought and understood.

My speech was noted the next day in the *New York Post,* and I received many kind notes and phone calls. And yet in light of so many other people who had died or were dying from AIDS, my news was hardly dramatic. Ironically, on the day I went public, the papers were saturated with the story of the Simpson-Goldman murders.

I know too much about the disease to believe that any one thing is going to be the miracle cure. But I still hold out some hope. Right now, at a clinic down in Miami, they've been growing my T cells in a machine. One of the top AIDS specialists on the planet, Dr. Paula Sparti, spearheaded the program, which is based on the principle of autologous, self-generated cellular therapy. The theory is that a small quantity of your blood is taken, cleansed of affected T cells, then put in a machine where, through bioengineering, they grow T cells by the billions. When they are ready to start the therapy, I will be one of the first people who try it. If it works, they'll need a spokesperson, a good fund raiser. And I know plenty of rich people who would donate their good money to the cause. These are people whom I could look directly in the eyes, saying, "You need to remove a hundred thousand dollars from your checking account. I know you were planning to bid on that eighteenth-century armoire. But this is for a worthy cause."

Living with AIDS becomes a full-time job, for which *you,*

the victim, pay a great deal of money. And you spend a great deal of time trying to keep up with things. It's difficult to live with the idea that your life is not fixable, to go through a day knowing that there is a multitude of bacteria and viruses that live relatively benignly in a healthy human body but that in your own body could suddenly turn violent and lethal. I find myself living in a world of acronyms: AZT (a drug), PCP (deadly pneumonia), MAC (a virulent bacterial infection), and on and on.

Now, twice a day, in the morning and at bedtime, I take a plastic tray divided into compartments and put it on my lap. The tray, which is a fishing-tackle box, is full of pills. There are so many pills to take: antifungus, antitoxoplasmosis, anti-pneumonia—it's hard to remember all of them. And if ever I confide to anyone that I'm worried about turning forgetful, about losing my mental faculties, I'm told that just remembering which pills I have and have not taken in any given day is enough of an intellectual task to disprove such a fear.

AIDS is the type of disease where you have to empower yourself, because when you don't have an immune system you can die of practically everything. In this way it's different from, say, breast cancer and prostate cancer—and I'm not saying it's worse—which are specifically life-threatening and can be dealt with specifically. With AIDS, there are so many potential but unproved protocols, so many unpaved avenues one can take. And it's hard to rely completely on the knowledge of one doctor; you have to advance your own learning curve, keep your ear to the ground to hear about new treatments.

My friend Ron English, who was once the head of the Community Research Initiative, an organization staging clinical trials for unapproved new therapies, is one of those people who have been battling AIDS for ten years, a long-term survivor type, who has tried everything. He's been there, he's done it all. He's a good source to call and say, "What do you think the efficacy is of X?" And he'll say, "Oh, I tried that five years ago. Here's the scoop." Doctors these days are usually very open about trying new things. They know that the reaction to the disease of each individual is as unique as his or her fingerprints. There are people who die very quickly. There are people who have lived for years with zero T cells.

One of the most wrenching parts of living with AIDS is when friends call with a complementary therapy that they are certain is going to help me. Although I am generally skeptical about such things, I hate disappointing them, and oftentimes I'll try something to make them happy. My friend Francine LeFrak insisted that I get in touch with the Welin sisters, who send Kambucha mushrooms around for free. These ladies also send along very specific printed instructions on how to grow the mushrooms, how to brew them into tea. Kambucha is a flat mushroom that is grown under wraps for seven to ten days. And when you take off the wrapping, it has grown another complete mushroom layer. It's inexorably hardy. Right now, Kambucha tea is gurgling away in a large Revere Ware soup pot in my kitchen. I've been drinking it for over a month, but I still don't see any change.

I'm sitting in the room that was once the aviary. It is a brilliant winter afternoon, and the room is awash with light. I haven't gone out very much in the last week. When people call with invitations, I respond, "Put me down as a 'definite maybe.' " The same goes with being an auctioneer at charity events—I do them if I feel up to it. This is my life as a definite maybe.

My energy seems to be flagging. Last night when I was doing an auction benefit, I found that my hands were shaking as I held the note card and read the description of the lot I was auctioning. The lot was a fantasy: the innocent pleasure of somebody's companionship for an evening. The lot was a young man flushed with health, a man kissed with beauty.

Epilogue

I'm back at Sotheby's again for an evening sale. I'm wearing a sapphire-blue evening jacket and I sit behind the auctioneer's podium in a white Queen Anne wing chair that is big enough for two people. It is June 26, 1995, and there is an auction going on in my honor to benefit four AIDS-related groups: Community Research Initiative on AIDS (CRIA), Friends in Deed, Gay Men's Health Crisis (GMHC), and God's Love We Deliver. It is probably the first time that one benefit auction has simultaneously assisted several different AIDS organizations.

Tonight I don't have the strength to do the live auction of eighty lots, and it only takes five auctioneers to replace me. I hover over the proceedings and pontificate, either embarrassing friends into bidding or admonishing those who have stopped. One friend of mine is bidding on a lot that I have offered: dinner for fifty at my home with Jean-Paul Gaultier. When my friend stops bidding, I say, "But aren't you a Dupont?"

"You didn't come here tonight to get a bargain," I remind everyone in the audience.

Many of the lots are from my own art collection, including paintings, porcelain, some silver, and a pile of cuff links. Mike

Nichols very generously offers a small walk-on part in his forth-coming film, *All the Pretty Horses,* which is auctioned for $7,000. Elton John donates his services as a songwriter for the highest-bidding prospective lyricist. That lot goes for $40,000. A Richard Avedon portrait of the highest bidder's children is auctioned for $18,000. A walk-on role in the TV sitcom *Melrose Place* is sold for $10,000. The total proceeds of the benefit—including private donations—come to $1.3 million.

The auction came close to fulfilling a fantasy I have had for some time and which some of my friends find spooky and morbid. For a long time now I've wanted to have an auction of my belongings, which would be like attending my own funeral. As I've never had to send any of my dogs to college, I've been able to accumulate a great many things over the years. I need to provide for the fact that I cannot take any of them with me. Outside of a small number of private bequests, I will ensure that each object goes to the person who desires it most. For me that's better than bequeathing paintings and *objets de vertu* to friends and family who may never look at them again.

My own private fantasy auction is a festive, formal affair with the men in black and the women in evening gowns. I stand on the podium as all my belongings are brought out on the stage and I sell them off one by one. I sell the painting of Sappho in my dining room, I sell my Persian rugs, I sell the silver ingot that I bought at the Warhol sale, the French and English furniture that I have collected throughout my lifetime. Of course one wants to live on in the memory of others, but I see myself living on through the diaspora of my objects that will go on to live for many centuries, particularly if they are carefully tended by their subsequent owners. I will even find it comforting to know whom they will belong to next.

Of course, there will be lots of competition for every single object. The proceeds will go to people with AIDS who do not have the luxury of dying in the style to which I'm accustomed. I'm not looking to canonize myself, however—I'm glad to help a good cause if I can. Because the fact remains that I love to sell in front of a crowd. I love the fevered attention of people who are waiting for their heart's desire to appear on the stage next to where I'm standing. I love to watch the face of an ardent collector preparing to make the final bid. I love the sound of sighs and murmurs when the price goes beyond anyone's expectation. And I love the silence that falls when I say, "Going once."

Acknowledgments

I'm really very grateful to Joseph Olshan, who helped me enormously, and to Eric Steel, who introduced us.

Lynn Nesbit, of Janklow & Nesbit, gave me advice and donated her fee to Gay Men's Health Crisis. She is a very classy lady.

John Marion, the recently retired chairman of Sotheby's North America, has helped and supported me (even when I was fractious) through my twenty-seven years in the business.

Dede Brooks, the president of Sotheby's Holdings worldwide, has been nervous about this memoir for two years. She was the first to read the manuscript and was hardly difficult. She is one of the best human beings I know. And her support of me at Sotheby's has been unmitigated. I love her for it.

My assistant, Tim Hamilton, I thank for putting up with me for over four years.

I have serious thanks to give to the talented and remarkable David Seidner, for the cover photograph of this book. He also donated his fee to GMHC. He's a mensch and a good friend.

David Seidner and Hoffman Props donated their time making and setting up the jacket.

I have also donated my fee and all royalties to GMHC, where I serve as a board member.

Not enough can be said about my best friend and care partner, David Jackson. I am always grateful and lucky to have David in my life. "You are the joy of my life. Thank you. I love you."

May 1995   R.W.

Index

Photo Credits

1, 12, 13, 14: Helaine Messer

2, 3, 4, 5, 10, 15, 16, 18, 19, 20, 21, 22, 23: Collection of the author

6, 7: Sotheby's

8: Norman McGrath

9: Andy Levin/Black Star

11: Ted Curry

17: Anita and Steve Shevett

24, 25: David S. Vaughan

26: Mary Hillard